· CONCISE GUIDE TO ·

Medications and Supplements for the Horse

Also by David W. Ramey, D.V.M.

Horsefeathers: Facts Versus Myths About Your Horse's Health

Concise Guide to Tendon and Ligament Injuries in the Horse

Concise Guide to Colic in the Horse

Concise Guide to Navicular Syndrome in the Horse

· CONCISE GUIDE TO ·

Medications and Supplements for the Horse

David W. Ramey, D.V.M.

Howell Book House
New York

Howell Book House
A Simon & Schuster Macmillan Company
1633 Broadway
New York, NY 10019

MACMILLAN is a registered trademark of Macmillan, Inc.

Library of Congress Cataloging-in-Publication Data

Ramey, David W.
        Concise guide to medications and supplements for the horse/David W. Ramey.
                p.   cm.
        Includes bibliographical references and index.
        ISBN 0-87605-916-7
        1. Horses—Diseases—Chemotherapy.   2. Horses—Feeding and feeds.
3. Veterinary drugs.   4. Feed additives.   I. Title.
SF951.R23 1995   95-25006
636.1'08951—dc20   CIP

Manufactured in the United States of America

10 9 8 7 6 5

CONTENTS

ACKNOWLEDGMENTS

Trying to collect all the information needed to write this handbook was a monumental task. Fortunately, Bebe Cunningham came to my rescue with excellent reference information regarding substances used to manufacture pharmaceuticals. Trying to make sure that the information presented was in a useful and understandable format was no less of a challenge. The still "beautiful and brilliant" Patricia Friedland and my secretary and right arm, Sandra Sudduth, made great suggestions and picked up errors that would have otherwise obscured the information in this book. Finally, Beth Lippitt, my fiancée, was a constant source of help, encouragement and support. The road ahead looks good.

INTRODUCTION

The horse is a surprisingly sturdy creature and a marvel of engineering. He is a large system, one that possesses tremendous strength and endurance but that is able to function on just vegetable material and water. Left to their own devices, horses do pretty well.

Of course, horses are not left to their own devices. Once man found out that horses made great work animals, play partners and companions, it was inevitable that things would begin to happen to the horse. Man seems to have a peculiar inability to leave well enough alone. Good enough rarely is. What this means for horses is that people who own them want to help them to be the best that they can be (sometimes maybe even better than they can be).

In most cases, this desire to help the horse is a good thing. For example, when your horse has an infection, helping him by giving him antibiotics to kill the infection is a fairly straightforward concept.

There is a difference, however, between helping a horse get back to what he was and trying to make a horse be better than what he is. In an attempt to do the latter, many things are done to or given to horses to enhance performance, increase efficiency (whatever that means) or merely to improve their appearance.

For example, a wide variety of nutrients can be demonstrated to be necessary in the normal diet of the horse. However, just because some of something is good does not mean that more of that same thing is necessarily better. For instance, iron is unquestionably needed by the horse for normal red blood cell formation. But more iron than what's required by the horse doesn't cause more red blood cells to be produced; in fact, too much iron can be toxic.

Frequently, the things that people do to "improve" their horses involve giving or applying one of a variety of medications and supplements that are marketed to the horse owner over the counter. Most of these products are, fortunately, fairly benign. Many of them actually do what they claim to do (supply vitamins and minerals, for example). However, many of the claims made by the manufacturers of medications and supplements are so vague and general that it's difficult to figure out what, if anything, they are supposed to do.

For the purposes of this book, a drug is defined as a substance that is used in the diagnosis, treatment or prevention of a disease. These substances are recognized and defined by the United States Food, Drug and Cosmetic Act. Their effects have been studied and their levels in blood and various tissues have been measured by scientists. Importantly, if a drug is given to an animal, its effect is usually predictable and controllable. Drugs are most commonly obtained by prescription or from your veterinarian. Their distribution and use is therefore, ideally, controlled.

Supplements, on the other hand, are a whole different ball game. Supplements are given to horses in an effort to "make up" deficiencies or to make the horse "better." Whether it be the composition of the hoof, the thickness of the hair or the overall sense of well-being that the horse is supposed to have, there are products out there that supposedly can help improve it. Importantly, supplements *are not* carefully regulated or measured for their ability to do what the manufacturer says that they will do.

Supplements, at least those that are manufactured by large companies, are usually safe for your horse. However, there is generally little or no controlled data as to their effectiveness.

There are many anecdotal reports about supplements, however. That is, there are stacks of testimonials of this trainer saying something is great or that horse owner saying, "Thank you for your product!" Anecdotes are no substitute for scientific investigation. Millions of dollars are spent by the horse-owning public on these products. Supplements are unlikely to hurt your horse; they may not help, either.

That being said, all you, the horse owner, really care about is doing the best that you can for your horse. Presumably, you will be somewhat curious about all the things you are going to be told that you should or must give to your horse. After all, just because you want to do *something* for your horse doesn't mean that you want to do just anything.

The purpose of this book is to help satisfy that curiosity. It is not intended to be a text on pharmacology (although some pharmacology is inevitable when dealing with the subject of drugs). Please note that the drugs listed in the book are generally identified by their generic names in order to avoid having to list all the different products separately; likewise, the ingredients of various supplements should be looked for under the headings for their ingredients. Where the proprietary name for a drug is used commonly (such as Banamine, which is a trademarked name that Schering-Plough Pharmaceuticals uses to market flunixin meglumine in the United States), the reader is usually referred to the generic heading. But to give you a hand in finding them, at the end of the book is an index of brand names described in the book.

This book is also not intended to be a catalogue of all the medications and supplements available for the horse. That would be impossible, as new products seem to appear almost daily. But by using this book to look for the ingredients listed on the product labels, you should be able to get an idea of what's in most of the products commonly used on horses and what they might actually do.

One other thing to remember. Research is going on constantly. Companies develop and release products prior to a full investigation of their effects. Drugs and supplements may be *safe* for horses but are released for use prior to completely understanding what they do. This is particularly true for drugs and supplements used for the treatment of tendon injuries, ligament problems and arthritis. In most cases, since there is so much new information, this means that there is no consensus in the veterinary community as to the "right" or "best" way to use a particular medication. There are many opinions as to "optimum" treatments and all of them may have some element of truth. Thus, you should rely on the experience of your veterinarian in selecting appropriate treatments for any condition of your horse that requires medical therapy. Of course, in medicine, as in life, nothing works the first time, every time.

If you believe everything that you read on product labels, this book is most likely not for you. An endless variety of beneficial claims are made for products sold for the horse (especially over-the-counter products) whether or not there is any evidence to substantiate them. If you choose to take the manufacturer's claims at face value, remember: Buyer beware.

This book *is* intended to help answer the cares and concerns of horse owners who are interested in many of the medications and supplements available for their horses. It explains why these substances are given, how (or if) they work and whether they have significant side effects. Ideally, then, if you do try to make your horse better, at least you will have some insight that will help you make a more educated decision regarding your horse's health. You will both be better for it.

CHAPTER I

Medications and Supplements: An Overview

As IMPORTANT AS WHICH DRUG YOU GIVE YOUR HORSE IS the route by which it is given. Drugs are most commonly given to the horse by one of three routes: oral, intramuscular or intravenous. (A few drugs are applied to the surface of something; this is called topical drug administration. Where applicable, this route is mentioned when the drug is discussed.)

No route of administration is always "better" than another. Each route, however, has its own characteristic way of being absorbed into the horse's system. Each route has its own advantages. Each way of giving a drug is somewhat different from the others.

Most drugs can only be given by one route. If given by a route other than that recommended, drugs that are otherwise safe can be dangerous. For example, the liquid preparation of phenylbutazone ("bute"), a commonly used anti-inflammatory agent, must be given intravenously. If it is given in the muscle, bute causes muscle irritation and abscesses because the solution is very irritating and acidic. Therefore, drugs should generally be given by the route recommended by the manufacturer (although your veterinarian may know of a safe alternative route for some drugs). Like most other things in life, you're generally better off if you follow the instructions.

INTRAVENOUS ADMINISTRATION

The intravenous (IV) route of administration puts a drug into the horse's system rapidly. It is generally used when a quick response is needed, such as in emergency situations or for inducing anesthesia or tranquilization. When given in the vein, a drug reaches a higher level in the system at a more rapid rate than if it is given by one of the other routes. A drug is also removed from the system more rapidly when it is given IV. The preparations of a drug given intravenously must be sterile (free of contamination or microorganisms) to avoid a generalized infection in the horse receiving the drug.

Intravenous injections are most commonly given in the jugular vein, on the side of the horse's neck. Intravenous administration of a drug is not particularly difficult (once you know how) but it is important that it be done properly. Significant side effects can occur when an IV injection is done improperly. For example, if the injected substance is accidentally deposited outside of the jugular vein, abscesses, swellings and soreness can occur. These problems from injection outside the vein can be serious enough in their own right. However, in addition, an even more serious and possibly permanent side effect, partial paralysis of the cartilage of the larynx ("roarer"), can also result from a missed IV injection.

In the back of the horse's mouth is the opening to the windpipe (trachea). The opening is guarded by the two cartilages of the larynx, known as the arytenoid cartilages. Muscles attached to these cartilages pull them open when the horse is breathing. The cartilages close when the horse swallows (this prevents food from going down into the lungs).

By some quirk of equine anatomy, the nerve that brings feeling and movement to the muscles of the cartilages on the left side of the larynx runs just alongside the left jugular vein, in a groove on the side of the horse's neck. By some quirk of *human* anatomy, most people are right-handed. Right-handers usually find it easier to make intravenous injections into the left jugular vein. If a substance is accidentally injected next to (instead of into) the vein, swelling and inflammation can result. The tissue irritation thus induced by the misplaced substance can envelop the nerve. This can damage the nerve or destroy it. Destruction of the nerve may result in a paralysis of the left arytenoid cartilage. (Incidentally, the nerves to the right side of the larynx are different. Injection into the right jugular vein does not pose the same potential problems as does injection into the left vein).

When a horse has this left laryngeal paralysis, he frequently begins to make noise ("roaring") when he exercises. This is because the paralysis prevents the airway from opening completely. Instead of opening up all the way, the paralyzed cartilage just hangs in the airway and vibrates (exactly like the paper in a kazoo). This is not dangerous to the horse but it can result in decreased performance.

An air passage obstructed by a paralyzed cartilage can reduce or stop the flow of air to the horse. Normal airway function is particularly important for racehorses. Racehorses need to have their airways completely open when they run. They need to get as much air into their lungs as possible when they are running at full speed. Show horses that are affected with a cartilage paralysis tend not to have problems getting enough air to breathe because they don't exercise nearly as hard as do the racing horses. However, the loud noise that is often made at exercise may be deemed undesirable in these animals.

Partial paralysis of the cartilages of the larynx generally does not get better on its own. The only treatment for the condition is surgery to "tie back" the paralyzed cartilage.

Another, even more serious complication of a misplaced intravenous injection again relates to the horse's anatomy. The jugular vein runs over the top of another important blood vessel, the carotid artery. The jugular vein carries blood back to the heart. The carotid artery, however, is carrying blood from the heart directly to the horse's brain. When a substance is given in the horse's vein, it has time to be diluted in the large volume of horse's blood. The substance mixes in the blood as it passes through the horse's heart and lungs. The now diluted substance is then distributed to the rest of the body.

If a drug is accidentally given into the carotid artery, however, it goes straight to the brain, minimally diluted. Direct delivery to the brain of a concentrated solution of a drug can knock a horse down to the ground or even kill him.

Obviously, then, it's important to be careful when giving an intravenous injection. Though it seems obvious, you do need to make sure that the drug is actually given in the vein.

INTRAMUSCULAR DRUG ADMINISTRATION

Drugs given in the muscle are absorbed more slowly than those given in the vein. When a drug is given intramuscularly (IM), the highest level of drug attained in the bloodstream is usually less than what can be reached by the intravenous route. However, drug levels for drugs given IM usually stay in the system for a longer time than those given IV. This can be an advantage in treatment of some conditions.

Intramuscular injections are more easily given than IV injections, especially when the horse getting the shot is a bit fractious or unruly.

Certain preparations, such as procaine penicillin, can only be given by IM injection. Like preparations for IV injection, IM products must also be sterile.

If you're not careful, it is possible to accidentally give an intravenous injection when intending to give an intramuscular one. When a needle is placed in the muscle, the end of it can come to rest inside a blood vessel (muscles are full of blood vessels). It is therefore important to pull back on the plunger of the syringe used to give the injection prior to pushing it in. You want to make sure that you don't see any blood being sucked back into the syringe when you pull back on the plunger (which would indicate the needle is in a vein). Intramuscular drugs such as procaine penicillin can be deadly if given intravenously.

Intramuscular injection is properly done directly into the large muscles of the neck or the big muscle groups of the hindquarters. The drug is then rapidly removed from the muscle by the horse's circulatory system. If a drug is accidentally given *between* muscle groups (in a fascial plane) it may not be well absorbed, however. Injection between muscles may also result in swellings or abscesses. Therefore it is recommended that intramuscular injections not be given high up on the neck, towards the head. It is much easier to get an injection between the many groups of small muscles that occur in that area than it is if the injection is given lower in the neck.

Occasionally, inevitably, horses develop abscesses or swellings from intramuscular injections. If an injection abscess forms, it tries to open to the outside of the horse and drain. Abscesses always expand toward the area of least resistance (the skin) and in the direction of the pull of gravity.

In anticipation of injection abscesses, even though the muscles are large, IM injection into the muscles of the hip is generally not recommended in horses. If an abscess from injection happens on the hip, in the gluteal muscles, the abscess fluid can't travel up and out of the horse's body (away from the pull of gravity). Instead, gravity pulls the fluid *down* the leg (it "gravitates"). The abscess fluid may not find a spot to exit until it reaches a point quite low on the leg. The fluid must dissect its way all the way down through the muscle groups of the limb to get out. This can take a long time (up to several months). In the meantime, the horse may be very sore and lame.

ORAL DRUG ADMINISTRATION

Oral routes of drug administration are associated with virtually no bad side effects (as long as the substances given aren't toxic). Blood levels of drugs given orally reach much the same levels in the blood as do drugs given by intramuscular injection. One of the nice things about drugs given orally is that they do not have to be sterile.

Even though oral drug administration is safe and effective, it is not necessarily easy in the horse. Since horses can be pretty discriminating eaters, attempting to give a drug orally by hiding it in the feed can be quite frustrating. Some horses are expert at sifting through their feed. These picky eaters are able to leave a neat little pile of medication in the feeder after they are finished eating the feed in which their medication was "hidden." No amount of molasses, honey or pancake syrup can kill the "bad" taste of some medications for finicky horses.

Consequently, a number of medications have been formulated into pastes that stick inside the horse's mouth. However, since horses can also be pretty fussy about having things put in their mouths, this isn't necessarily the answer, either. Paste medications can be squirted into (and sometimes spit right back out of) the horse's mouth. This same problem can be seen in trying to give a horse a liquid medication or in attempting to place pills in the back of his throat. Even though there are a lot of effective ways to medicate a horse, sometimes there is no easy way.

DRUG DOSAGE

It is always important to follow the recommended dosage schedule of any drug given to your horse. The dosage schedule is affected by a number of factors, including how rapidly the drug is removed from the system, what level of the drug needs to be maintained in the system for it to be effective and what effect is desired. (For example, it may be desirable to have a horse more or less tranquilized, depending on what you want to do to the horse.)

For drugs to be effective, their dosage schedules must be followed closely. A dosage schedule of three times a day is more properly stated as every eight hours; giving a three-times-a-day medication at eight o'clock in the morning, at noon and at six in the evening may result in drug levels that are too high at some times and nonexistent at others. Making sure that your horse gets his drugs at the right time may require some dedication from you. Your veterinarian should advise you as to the proper dosage schedule for drugs.

In addition to the proper dosage interval, the proper dose of a drug should also be followed. Drugs are not harmless (nor are they generally dangerous). Drugs that are safe at one dose may be dangerous at twice the dose. For this reason, you should not automatically assume that, just because your horse is not getting better as quickly as you think he should, by increasing the dose you will help him get better faster (the "bigger hammer" theory).

In fact, doubling the dose of a drug does not necessarily increase its effectiveness. A doubled dose may not even dramatically increase the time that a particular dose will stay in the system. This is because of what is known as the half-life of a drug.

When a drug is put into the horse's system, it immediately begins to be removed as a result of the horse's normal metabolic functions. Pharmacologists measure the time it takes for half of the initial dose to be removed from the horse's system. This is called the half-life of the drug. It gives pharmacologists a useful measure of the length of time that a particular drug may be effective in the horse's system.

If you double the dose of a drug, you increase its duration in the system by one half-life. If the half-life of a particular drug is four hours, by doubling the dose you thus only increase the length of time that a single dose of the drug is in the system by that much time. However, while doubling the dose of a drug may not significantly prolong the time that the drug is in the system, doubling the dose can *significantly* increase the potential for adverse side effects. You should always check with your veterinarian before altering the dose of any prescribed drug from that which is recommended.

DRUG LABELLING:
LIMITATIONS AND APPLICATIONS

Not all drugs used in horses have been specifically tested on horses. Veterinarians have broad authority in prescribing drugs for horses. It is tremendously difficult to bring a drug to market through the morass of testing procedures required by the U.S. Food and Drug Administration. Each drug has to be tested for each species in which it is to be used and for each specific use for which a benefit is claimed. This can be extremely expensive for the drug companies. Thus, not all drugs that are used in horses have been specifically approved for use in them, nor are all the drugs given to horses used according to the label directions.

For example, the label directive "Not for use in horses intended for food" is put there so that companies don't have to do testing for drug residues in horses that may end up entering the food chain. Rather than pay for the testing, they tell you not to use the drug in these horses. Similarly, gentamycin sulfate, a commonly used antibiotic, is approved for use in the uterus of mares only. However, the drug is frequently given in the muscle to treat bacterial infections of various areas. The company that makes gentamycin didn't want to pay for the testing to see if the drug is safe for horses when given in the muscle, so they put a restrictive label on it. Nonetheless, veterinarians have used gentamycin sulfate for years in a manner other than that which is directed on the label. It has been found to be safe and effective. Veterinarians have wide discretion in trying to make use of any drug available that can potentially help sick horses. They usually know what you can and cannot do. They are the ones to ask about drugs.

All drugs are potentially toxic substances. Paracelsus (1493–1541) was a Swiss doctor who was the first to suggest that disease occurred as a result of some specific cause outside the body. He noted, "All substances are poisons, for there is nothing without poisonous qualities. It is only the dose which makes a substance poisonous." After correct diagnosis and when given in the proper dosage and by recommended routes of administration, drugs are likely to produce beneficial effects. They should be used accordingly.

OVER-THE-COUNTER MEDICATIONS

Equine health care is complicated by the fact that there are a tremendous number of over-the-counter medications sold to horse owners. Concerned horse owners are usually trying to make their horses "better," with or without the aid of professional veterinary care. Such efforts are roughly akin to prescribing home remedies for yourself (or your friends).

Sometimes, over-the-counter medications seem to work. For example, if you have a cold, most of the time you'll eventually be just fine no matter what treatment you prescribe for yourself. This is because the body has a tremendous capacity and urge to heal itself. Most problems do get better. Sometimes medications get the credit for healing which would have occurred anyway. However, if you have a serious problem such as pneumonia, over-the-counter medications aren't likely to do much good in curing it.

Over-the-counter medications for horses make a wide variety of claims as to their effectiveness. Their claims are, by necessity, very general and vague. If over-the-counter medications made specific claims about their effectiveness, they would be subject to the same rules and regulations that confront the manufacturers of pharmaceutical products. They would be regulated by the United States Food and Drug Administration. Drug manufacturers have to go through a variety of steps to make sure that their products are safe and that they actually do what they claim to do. Manufacturers of over-the-counter medications do not have to follow these rules, as long as they do not make specific claims. Therefore, the specific effects of many supplement products are poorly understood, if they are understood at all.

SUPPLEMENTS

By definition, a supplement is something that is provided to complete something, to make up for a deficiency or to extend or strengthen the whole (*American Heritage Dictionary of the English Language*, 3rd ed., Boston:

Houghton Mifflin Company, 1992). Supplements that are provided to the horse's diet purport to do most or all of these things.

Supplementing for "Deficiencies"

Probably the most common deficiency seen in the horse is a deficiency in energy, that is, an inadequate amount of calories in the diet. Horses are often not given enough feed for the work that is required of them. Work such as exercise, lactation or growth requires a lot of energy. Horses that work hard may need more feed than what is routinely given to them. However, there are many supplements available that claim to "help" the horse with deficiencies in energy; most contain a variety of vitamins, minerals or proteins.

The problem with most energy-deficient horses, however, is not so much a lack of supplements as it is a lack of proper feeding. Horses that are energy deficient lose weight, are in poor condition and lack energy. Horses lacking in calories in the diet are not helped by any amount of supplemental vitamins or minerals.

People being people, however, generally overlook a lack of feed as a cause of a lack of energy and weight loss in their horse. Finding out that your horse is losing weight because he's not getting enough to eat is sort of like finding out that your washing machine doesn't work because you forgot to plug it in. You're happy to find out what the problem is, but it's kind of embarrassing and you'd really rather it be something else. With horses, this generally means that horse owners first start looking to areas other than the feed as potential causes of their horse's weight loss or lack of energy.

In fact, horses are rarely deficient in anything besides energy. It is very difficult to create a diet of normal horse feed that supplies enough calories for their systems to run but that is also deficient in protein, vitamins and minerals. Vitamins, minerals and protein all have important functions in the horse. However, providing more of any of these substances than what is needed for a particular function will not cause the horse to do that function better. Nor are vitamins and minerals necessarily benign. In fact, toxicities of vitamins and minerals have been reported in the horse (though rarely).

Dietary protein supplements are also commonly given to horses by their well-meaning owners. Unquestionably, the horse needs protein to build the body's tissues. However, extra dietary protein taken in by the horse is not beneficial (nor is it harmful). Nor do protein requirements in horses go up when they exercise. Excess protein is merely digested by the horse and converted to energy. Protein supplements are just relatively expensive sources of supplemental energy for the horse.

Supplementing to "Strengthen" the Horse

The other defined function of supplements is to complete or strengthen the whole (horse). In this regard, supplements are commonly turned to in efforts to "improve" the horse, or to make him "better," at least in the mind of the owner. This generally means that the owner wants the horse to be better than or somehow different from the way he actually is (this is a problem that plagues many relationships).

Consequently, a variety of supplements are available that claim a mind-boggling array of beneficial effects. The following is a list of claims that have been taken from advertisements for various feed supplements:

- "Improves overall bloom"
- "Improves disposition"
- "Better general health"
- "Lengthens attention span"

- "Increases mental stability"
- "Helps hyper horses come down and lackadaisical horses come up"
- "Significant improvement in comfort"
- "Improves digestion"

All of these claims are truly amazing, if only because they are almost impossible to understand. For example, a supplement may be promoted to "improve performance." In reality, since "performance" is such a vague concept and "improvement" is so subjective, such claims are difficult, if not impossible, to measure.

If specific claims were made for supplements ("This product is proven effective for the relief of pain and inflammation associated with chronic arthritis," for example), these substances would fall under all the rules and regulations that the manufacturers of drugs are subject to. Supplement manufacturers would have to prove that their products actually work if they were held to these standards. Since supplement manufacturers don't want to have to be held to the same standards as the drug manufacturers, they usually don't make specific claims as to the effectiveness or method of action of their products.

Supplements are also promoted by stating what the individual ingredients are in that supplement and how they are used in the horse. Then, either directly or by implication, the horse owner is led to believe that the horse may not be getting enough of that ingredient. For example, the statement "This supplement contains fourteen amino acids. If any one of them is deficient in the diet, the horse's protein needs will not be fulfilled" is undoubtedly true. However, protein or amino acid deficient diets are never reported as problems in the horse. Supplementation with amino acids is rarely, if ever, required. Similar examples can be given for vitamins, minerals and electrolytes, the other most commonly supplemented substances.

PRODUCT LABELLING

It is very important that you read the labels of supplements for your horse. You not only want to find out what the supplements are supposed to do, you want to find out what is in the supplements that is supposed to cause the beneficial effects. Some over-the-counter medications and supplements do not even carry a listing of ingredients! It seems, at best, foolish to use a product on your horse that will not reveal its ingredients. After all, your horse is relying on you to take care of him. If products don't care enough to tell you what you are giving to your horse, why should you care to use them?

If the supplement or over-the-counter medication that you use for your horse has chosen to list the ingredients, look for them under the various individual headings in this book. Then you can at least try to understand what, if any, beneficial effects can be expected for your horse when you give him these products.

CHAPTER 2

Medications and the Performance Horse

HORSES FIND THEMSELVES IN A VARIETY OF SPORTING competitions, such as racing, jumping, eventing, western events and dressage. Horses are athletes. Like all athletes, some will be better at their particular sport than others. Of course, people are rarely willing to accept the inherent natural limitations of an individual animal. Not only that, but in competitions almost everyone seems to be looking for an "edge" to make their horses just a little better. Accordingly, they may try to influence the horses' performance through various medications.

MEDICATIONS TO INCREASE PERFORMANCE

In some horses, medications are given in hopes that the horse's performance will be improved beyond what it would be without the medication. Examples of such medications might be stimulants such as amphetamines or narcotics, used in an effort to fire up racehorses. (Unlike their effects in people, narcotics tend to cause excitement in horses.) Similarly, vitamins or anabolic steroids are sometimes used in an attempt to make race or show horses "stronger" or more aggressive.

The effectiveness of stimulant medications in improving horse performance is not at all clear. When a horse is racing, he is being asked for an all-out, maximum effort. The idea of giving stimulants, then, is to put something into the horse that will make him do more than that which he is ordinarily capable of doing with his maximum effort. Whether this can be done is certainly questionable; after all, the horse can only do what he can do. No studies have shown that stimulant drugs have any effect on improving the performance of racehorses.

"Jugs" of fluids and vitamins or injections of such vitamins as cyanocobalamin (vitamin B-12) are commonly given to try to make horses more energetic or to increase their red blood cell count. However, the administration of vitamins before a race or a show certainly never has been shown to have any beneficial effect in horses. Treatments such as these have been consistently ineffective in causing any changes in horses that have received them. (Being somewhat expensive, these treatments *do* consistently make the horse owner somewhat poorer.)

On the other hand, anabolic steroids, another class of drugs purported to increase performance, at least have the *potential* to increase performance. These drugs can increase muscle mass. That is why they are used illegally by human weight lifters, football players and track stars. However, one study done in Scotland failed to show any increase in performance in racehorses given these drugs.

Anabolic steroids do have androgenic effects; that is, they may make horses demonstrate more aggressive, stallion-like behavior. For this reason, they are sometimes used in efforts to make horses that seem to lack energy act more aggressive. Again, however, the use of these drugs in this fashion has failed to yield reliable and consistent results.

MEDICATIONS TO DECREASE PERFORMANCE

In racehorses, medications such as tranquilizers or depressants may be given in an effort to calm nervous or "washy" horses that may expend lots of energy in the paddock prior to a race. If the horses are calmer in the paddock, it is hoped that they will run better during the race. Also, such drugs may be given to horses in an intentional effort to get them to lose races; a long shot that wins a race can bring a handsome profit to the bettor who knew beforehand that the favorite was tranquilized. Of course, the use of such medications for such purposes is strictly prohibited by racing commissions.

In show horses, substances that induce tranquilization and cannot be detected are sought after by some people. In order to win competitions, show hunters not only have to jump fences, they have to jump in a calm and happy fashion (at least the judges have to think that the horses are calm and happy). Unfortunately, calm and happiness may not necessarily be the nature of a particular horse. For some reason, the horse might actually prefer staying in his stall to being kicked around the ring and asked to jump over a bunch of obstacles. Medications may be given to the horse to help him overcome this completely rational "problem."

Exercise, in the form of precompetition lungeing, for example, is one method of trying to make a horse tired (and therefore quieter) prior to his classes. However, many veterinarians and trainers fear that additional exercise, beyond what the horse gets in the competition, may ultimately increase wear and tear on the horse. They feel that this could conceivably lead to injuries of the musculoskeletal system. (Not only that, but lungeing a horse prior to competition means that the trainer has to be up really early.) Therefore, other methods of making the horse relax are looked for. Medications that provide mild sedation and tranquilization of the horse are an easy and seductive alternative to solving the "problem" of the horse that doesn't appear to be calm and happy in the show ring. However, the use of tranquilizers (the obvious drug of choice for this "problem") in this fashion is a clear violation of the rules of various horse show associations. Many other substances which cannot be detected by routine drug tests are used to try to calm horses. Substances such as tryptophan, calcium, dexamethasone or ACTH have never shown any consistent effect of calming horses. The use of any sort of tranquilizing agent, detectable or otherwise, is clearly against the rules.

MEDICATIONS TO RESTORE PERFORMANCE

The use of medications to restore a horse's normal performance is certainly common. The rationale for this use of medication in this fashion is easy to understand. For example, if a horse is experiencing some form of minor pain, he may limp and be reluctant or unable to perform in a normal fashion. An anti-inflammatory and pain-relieving agent would be expected to help restore the horse's normal performance by helping to alleviate the pain; if the horse doesn't hurt, he will be more likely to perform "normally."

A number of medications are used in this fashion. Nonsteroidal anti-inflammatory agents, drugs that help relieve pain and inflammation, such as phenylbutazone, are among the drugs most commonly administered to horses. Similarly, if a horse's joint is sore and inflamed, injections of steroidal anti-inflammatory agents directly into the joint is a common way to help relieve inflammation and the resulting pain.

Medications such as the above are clearly therapeutic. They are just as clearly overused. For example, not all horses that compete will become sore or lame as a result. However, many competition horses are often given anti-inflammatory drugs "just in case" they get sore.

When horses compete, some people want to try to make sure that their horse has an edge on the competition. They also want to make sure that some other competitor doesn't have an "unfair" chemical advantage. Consequently, many competition horses end up floating in drugs that are supposed to "help" them perform in one way or another if for no other reason than "because everyone else is doing it." And what one person does, others seem to follow. It seems sometimes that if a successful trainer said that he was giving his horse a pint of motor oil every day, soon everyone in the area would be rushing to the auto parts store to stock up.

Local injections of steroidal anti-inflammatory agents into arthritic horse joints may allow the horse to continue to perform in the short term. However, continued indiscriminate use of steroids may be at the expense of the horse's future soundness (or life).

Some unethical horse people will even anesthetize arthritic joints so that the horse does not feel the damaged joint at all. This practice is clearly dangerous to the horse and to the rider. It can result in total breakdown of the horse, who may be unable to feel and thereby protect his leg. If the horse breaks down, the rider can also be seriously injured. Horse owners and trainers should consider the potential adverse consequences of unlimited or careless use of medications in horses.

Vitamin and mineral supplements are also commonly used to try to ensure that a horse is normal and in good health. While commonly used, no studies have shown that vitamin and mineral supplements are necessary or even beneficial.

Endurance horses are frequently supplemented with electrolytes. Electrolytes are body salts that are lost in the horse's sweat. Supplementation with electrolytes certainly does not appear to be harmful for these horses;

in fact, one study suggests that the administration of electrolytes, glucose and water in these horses may help delay fatigue. Providing adequate water, however, is the most important factor to consider for endurance horses.

In reality, getting optimum performance from your horse is not that complicated. The best thing that you can do for your horse to make sure that his performance is normal (and as good as is possible for him) is to feed him well and provide good care.

ACCIDENTAL MEDICATIONS

Some of the medications given to horses can cause them to test positive for the presence of substances in the blood that are considered illegal by the overseeing competition organizations. For example, injections of procaine penicillin, a commonly used antibiotic, will cause horses to test positive for the presence of illegal anesthetic agents. Procaine is an anesthetic agent added to penicillin to take the sting out of its injection. Unfortunately, it is impossible for a drug test to tell the difference between injections of an antibiotic for therapeutic purposes and an illegally administered local anesthetic. An anesthetic might be illegally given to make a sore area of the horse numb, so that he can compete without signs of lameness. Similarly, guaifenesin, used as an expectorant in some cough preparations, can cause a falsely positive drug test for methocarbamol, a muscle relaxant.

Sometimes horses will accidentally test positive for drugs if they are given some otherwise benign substance. For example, cola drinks or chocolate can cause a horse to test positive for caffeine, an illegal stimulant. Fortunately, this sort of thing doesn't happen very often.

When drugs are given to horses, the horse's system metabolizes them and removes them from the system. Depending on the drugs, this can take from a period of days to months. Therefore, substances that are prohibited by organizations that oversee competitions should be used carefully. The horse owner and trainer must pay attention and make sure that the horse has had adequate time to let the drug clear his system.

In horse shows overseen by the American Horse Shows Association (AHSA), one way to ensure that drug detection does not become a problem is to "declare" that a drug has been given to a horse for therapeutic purposes prior to competition. The horse will be able to show twenty-four hours after the declared last time of administration of the drug. If he then tests positive for some substance, you will not be subject to penalties.

MEDICATIONS TO "MASK" DRUGS OR DILUTE OTHER MEDICATIONS

Some medications are given to horses in an effort to make it more difficult to detect other, prohibited drugs. In past years, substances such as thiamine (vitamin B-I) and dipyrone have been used as "masking" agents. Strangely, these drugs have never been effective in preventing detection of other drugs.

Similarly, diuretics may be given to horses to avoid positive drug tests. Diuretics dilute the concentration of drugs in the urine by increasing the amount of water in it. However, this also is not a very effective way to get around drug tests. The effects of diuretics are quite rapid and transient, lasting only a few hours. The use of diuretics is generally controlled or prohibited by the various organizations.

THE REGULATION OF MEDICATIONS IN PERFORMANCE HORSES

Performance horses are subjected to a mind-numbing array of regulations, depending on the organization that oversees the competitions. It would be virtually impossible to detail all of the individual rules and regulations regarding the use of drugs and medications for each horse organization. Each organization has its own rules regarding the use of drugs and medications, and those rules are subject to constant modification. In the case of racehorses, the medication rules vary in each state (there are now forty-three states that have pari-mutuel racing).

Drug rules reflect the different philosophies of the various organizations. Bodies such as the Jockey Club, the Federation Equestre Internationale (FEI), the United States Equestrian Team and the American Quarter Horse Association (AQHA) are the most strict. Their view is that horses should not be in an event if they have detectable levels of any drug in their systems. At the other end of the spectrum, the National Cutting Horse Association (NCHA) and the National Reining Horse Association (NRHA) of the United States don't have any rules prohibiting the use of foreign substances in horses (although the NCHA does not allow the administration of any drugs to horses in the ring, except in emergency situations).

The use of most drugs in racehorses is prohibited. Most states have specific regulations that allow the use of phenylbutazone (and other nonsteroidal anti-inflammatory drugs) and furosemide. The states differ, however, in how they approach the problem of medication control.

In New York State, certain drugs may be given within a certain period of time prior to post. For example, antihistamines must not be given within forty-eight hours of post time.

In the state of California, the regulations are written specifically defining the permitted amounts or levels of drugs in the horse. These rules are similar to rules regarding blood alcohol levels in people; it doesn't really matter how much you had to drink or when you drank it—if your blood alcohol level is above the legal limit, you're sunk. It is literally impossible to know whether a particular horse's level of a particular drug will be within acceptable levels after a certain period of time without actually testing him to see. When a drug is given to a horse, it is removed from the system at a relatively constant rate. Importantly, this rate varies with the individual horse. Blood or urine levels of drugs such as phenylbutazone above those permitted may subject the owner and trainer to sanctions from the racing commission.

The state of Kentucky has yet another approach to the control of medication. Horses cannot run on tranquilizers, stimulants, depressants, local anesthetics or narcotics. All other drugs are considered therapeutic and their use is permitted under veterinary supervision.

The drug rules of the American Horse Shows Association, the largest regulatory body overseeing show horses in the United States, are the most complex of all of the organizations. The AHSA tests thousands of horses every year (and spends almost two million dollars a year doing so) in an effort to ensure that horse show competitions are fair. The rules of the AHSA are subject to constant review and change. It is important that competitors, trainers and veterinarians involved with show horses be aware of the changing and convoluted nature of the drug rules of the AHSA.

The AHSA categorizes drugs into one of three groups. Group one is substances that might affect performance. Group one drugs are those such as stimulants, tranquilizers and depressants. This group includes literally thousands of drugs (Table I).

Group two drugs are those substances that have quantitative restrictions. The AHSA restricts the amounts of these drugs that can be given to the horse. Group two drugs include such substances as phenylbutazone and flunixin meglumine, two of the most commonly used nonsteroidal anti-inflammatory drugs for the horse. (Interestingly, up to the time of publication of this book, there were no regulations concerning permissible levels of other nonsteroidal anti-inflammatory agents.) Methocarbamol, a muscle relaxant with sedative side effects, also has quantitative restrictions placed on it. The AHSA provides guidelines to competitors for the use of these drugs.

Group three drugs are substances that may interfere with laboratory procedures ("masking agents"). They are prohibited regardless of how harmless the drug might be or the purpose for which the drug was given. In 1995, this group of drugs was radically narrowed due to changes in the laboratory procedures of the AHSA. Now, the only drugs that are classified as masking substances are furosemide (Lasix) and other *potent* diuretics. (Some diuretics are considered not to be potent enough to cause any problems with drug detection). Drugs that previously fell into this category, such as sulfa antibacterial drugs, dipyrone and benzimidazole deworming products, are now allowed.

The AHSA does allow for exceptions to their rules when drugs are administered for therapeutic purposes. A therapeutic purpose is one that is considered necessary for the treatment of illness or injury. If a forbidden substance is used for a therapeutic purpose, the horse must be kept out of competition for twenty-four hours after the substance is given. A drug declaration form must also be filed within one hour after the drug was given or after arrival at the show grounds, if it was given prior to the start of a competition.

In the above exception, the definition of the word "therapeutic" is important. For example, the AHSA considers the use of tranquilizers such as acepromazine to aid in clipping, training or trailering horses to be a *nontherapeutic* use of these drugs. Filing drug declaration forms after drugs are used in a "nontherapeutic" manner is considered inappropriate and will not make it legal for the horse to compete.

It is very important that the individual competitor or trainer be familiar with the rules that apply to his or her particular sport in order to avoid disqualification or suspension from competition. For example, effective December 1, 1995, endurance horses competing under AHSA sanctions will not be allowed to have *any* detectable levels of drugs in their systems. Due to the sometimes vague and ever-changing nature of drug regulations, close consultation with your trainer, veterinarian and/ or overseeing competition body is strongly recommended. The best way to avoid problems regarding allowable levels of drugs in your performance horse is to know the rules.

TABLE I
EXAMPLES OF SUBSTANCES THAT ARE FORBIDDEN BY THE AHSA
DRUGS AND MEDICATIONS RULE

Acepromazine	Dextromethorphan	Isoxsuprine
Albuterol	Diazepam	Levallorphan
Aminophylline	Diphenhydramine	Levorphanol
Amphetamines	Dyphylline	Lidocaine
Atropine	Ephedrine	Mazindol
Azaperone	Etorphine	Mepivacaine
Benzocaine	Fentanyl	Methylphenidate
Caffeine	Fluphenazine	Morphine
Chlorpheniramine	Guaifenesin	Nikethamide
Chlorprothixene	Haloperidol	Oxymorphone
Clenbuterol	Homatropine	Pentazocine
Cocaine	Hydromorphone	Phenobarbital
Detomidine	Hydroxyzine	Phenylephrine

Continued on next page

TABLE I—*Continued*

Phenytoin	Propionylpromazine	Tetracaine
Piperacetazine	Propoxyphene	Theophylline
Prethcamide	Pyrilamine	Tripelennamine
Procaine	Reserpine	Tropicamide
Promazine	Strychnine	Xylazine

(Data from R. R. Gowen and J. G. Lengel, "Regulatory Aspects of Drug Use in Performance Horses," Vet Clin NA 9(3): 450, 1993.)

CHAPTER 3

Medications and Supplements for the Horse

· A ·

ABSORBINE *(see Liniment)*

ACEPROMAZINE MALEATE *("Ace") PromAce*

Acepromazine is a commonly prescribed tranquilizer for horses. Its effects are generally milder than other tranquilizers used in horses but somewhat longer lasting. There are reports of tranquilization lasting up to twenty-four hours in some horses (although most horses seem tranquilized for only a few hours).

Acepromazine is available in a sterile solution which may be given by IM or IV injection. It is also available in tablets. The sterile solution of acepromazine maleate has also been squirted in the mouth, where it can be absorbed through the mucous membranes of the gums. A related product, Promazine granules, is given in the feed (see Promazine Hydrochloride).

PRECAUTIONS   Tranquilization of horses with acepromazine may lead to a false sense of security when working around them. Horses that are tranquilized can still react quickly to external stimuli. Horses maintain their visual and hearing capacities while on acepromazine, so loud sounds or rapid movements should be avoided. The drug has little, if any, pain-relieving effect. Painful procedures should be avoided while using this drug.

Acepromazine is not a very potent tranquilizer. If a horse really objects to something, such as body clipping, acepromazine may not provide enough tranquilization to get the job done, no matter how much is used. To increase the tranquilizing effect, sometimes acepromazine is used in combination with other tranquilizers, such as xylazine or detomodine.

Horses intended for use in shows must not have traces of this drug in their systems. Recommended withdrawal time by the American Horse Shows Association (AHSA) is seventy-two hours prior to competition.

SIDE EFFECTS   In addition to its tranquilizing effects, acepromazine is a potent dilator of the small peripheral blood vessels of the horse's body. Because of this side effect, it is occasionally prescribed for the treatment of laminitis, in an effort to improve or increase circulation to the feet.

Acepromazine causes relaxation of the muscles of the penis in male horses. An unfortunate side effect, partial paralysis of the muscles of the penis, has been described. Horses so affected may be unable to retract their penis. Although this complication is *extremely* rare, this side effect may be a consideration if the drug is intended to be used in breeding stallions.

ACTH   *(Adrenocorticotropic Hormone)*

ACTH is a hormone that serves as a stimulator of the adrenal glands. The adrenal glands lie next to the kidneys (hence, the name "adrenal") and produce a number of hormones important for normal metabolic functions in the horse. ACTH is available as a sterile gel which is given by IM administration.

ACTH is manufactured as a diagnostic aid to help determine if there is some problem with adrenal gland function in dogs and cats. However, the drug is used in horses in an effort to stimulate the release of cortisol into the horse's body. Some people feel that higher levels of plasma cortisol ("natural" steroids) may make a horse feel calmer. There is no medical evidence to support this use of the drug and no studies have been done to document its effects.

Indiscriminate use of ACTH in horses is not advisable. There is a potential to exhaust or adversely affect the adrenal gland through its use in this fashion.

ADEQUAN   *(see Polysulfated Glycosaminoglycan)*

ALCOHOL

Alcohol is used primarily as a solvent, to dissolve other substances. It has a variety of pharmacologic uses.

As a solvent, alcohol can be used to remove things from the skin, such as tape residue or some oily substances. In people, it can be used to bathe the skin for the purpose of cooling it; it does this by evaporating quickly, causing a cooling effect. In high concentrations alcohol is an irritant to the skin.

In horses, alcohol is used to formulate a number of preparations such as liniments, wound treatments and hoof dressings. Some people apply alcohol directly to the horse's legs after exercise, presumably as some sort of liniment or coolant. What the actual effect of such a treatment might be is unknown.

Alcohol baths are recommended by some veterinarians in an attempt to reduce fever in sick horses. Due to its rapid evaporation and subsequent cooling effect, alcohol works well in this regard.

Alcohol is a good antiseptic (local anti-infective) for the skin; it kills bacteria by dehydrating them as the alcohol dries. However, swabbing the skin with alcohol prior to local injections does little apparent good unless the area is allowed to dry first; otherwise, the local skin bacteria in the swabbed area are merely suspended in a solution of alcohol. Thus, it may theoretically be easier to contaminate the underlying tissue if the skin over the area is swabbed with alcohol first. It may be easier to get bacteria under the skin if they're in solution than if they're only lying on the skin. In practice, it probably doesn't really matter if you swab an injection site with alcohol or not.

ALLANTOIN

In people, allantoin is used in an effort to promote healing and tissue repair. It is used in the treatment of various skin conditions such as wounds and skin infections. In World War I, it was noticed that wounds that were infested with maggots healed better than those that had no maggot infestation; the maggots were discovered to produce allantoin.

Allantoin is available as an ingredient in an over-the-counter hoof dressing.

ALMOND OIL

Almond oil is obtained by pressing almonds. It has some use as an emollient (see Emollients). Almond oil is contained in some hoof dressings (see Hoof Dressings).

ALOE VERA

There are over two hundred varieties of plants that produce aloes, a sticky juice obtained from the leaves. Aloe vera is a common house plant. The juice from this plant is commonly applied to cuts and burns, where it is reported to have emollient effects (see Emollients). It is also reported to speed healing. Plant aloes are used as cathartics (stimulants to the intestines that cause evacuation of the bowels) in people.

In the 1960s, in Japan, a study was done that suggested that aloe could speed healing of damaged skin. More recently, study groups from the U.S. Food and Drug Administration have looked at the tests done on aloe and concluded that there is no good evidence for this.

Aloe vera is commonly applied to wounds of the horse and is available in a number of over-the-counter preparations for this purpose. It is also found in some hoof dressing products.

ALTRENOGEST   *Regumate*

Altrenogest is a progestin. Progestins are used to prevent estrus ("heat") in mares and in the management of breeding mares.

To prevent estrus, altrenogest is commonly used in show mares, to keep them from coming into heat (with all its behavioral side effects) during competition.

In the management of broodmares, altrenogest has been used in attempts to "synchronize" breeding cycles (that is, to try to get mares to come into heat at particular times). Altrenogest is also used to help regulate "transitional" mares. Mares have a breeding season; that is, there is a time that they can be bred and a time when they do not come into heat. Frequently, when their heat cycle begins and ends, it is irregular, with unpredictable patterns of prolonged heat. Altrenogest has been used to modulate this activity and to encourage the beginning of a more normal heat cycle (see Progesterone).

Some people have advocated the use of altrenogest to try to alter the mood of unruly male horses, too. There is no clinical data to support this use of the drug; however, it seems to have little chance of being harmful to males.

PRECAUTIONS   Altrenogest can be absorbed through human skin. It therefore has the potential to affect the menstrual cycle of women administering the drug. Latex gloves should be worn to protect the hands and prevent skin absorption. Pregnant women should not handle altrenogest.

SIDE EFFECTS   Altrenogest is remarkably safe and associated with no significant side effects. Neither altrenogest nor any other progestin should be used in mares that have previously had or are currently exhibiting signs of uterine infection or inflammation because it may make the problem worse.

ALUM

Alum has been around since the days of the Greeks. Alum is a powerful astringent and has mild antiseptic properties (see Astringent, Antiseptic). Human athletes use it to toughen their skin. It is also used to stop blood flow. Alum is a principal component of styptic pencils, used to stop bleeding after people cut themselves shaving.

In horses, alum is found in some wound dressings, where it is presumably used to help stop or prevent surface bleeding.

ALUMINUM SULFATE

Aluminum sulfate is a powerful astringent, much like alum (see Alum, Astringent). It is widely used to make antiperspirant products for people.

Aluminum sulfate is a component of a coolant gel available for use on horse legs (see Coolant Gel). Presumably its astringent effects may make the skin of the leg seem "tighter." It is unlikely to have any other effects on the horse's leg.

AMIKACIN SULFATE *Amiglyde-V*

Amikacin is one of a group of antibiotics known as the aminoglycosides. Amikacin comes as a sterile solution that can be administered by IM or IV injection. It is also commonly used to treat intrauterine infections in mares. Amikacin is resistant to most of the enzymes that bacteria produce that inactivate other drugs of the same class.

PRECAUTIONS   Amikacin is an effective drug when used as directed. However, its use is limited because of the cost of the drug. The drug can be used in show horses that are at competitions.

SIDE EFFECTS   Aminoglycoside antibiotics (like amikacin) have two primary side effects that have been described. First, they can damage the centers of hearing and balance in the brain. Second, they may impair function of the kidneys. Although these side effects are rare, horses that have suspect kidney function (such as those that are dehydrated) or that are very young with immature kidneys should be monitored closely if this drug is chosen to treat an infection. Care should be taken when amikacin is used with nonsteroidal anti-inflammatory drugs because of the increased potential for kidney-related side effects.

AMINO ACID

Amino acids are the building blocks from which proteins are made (proteins are the structural components that make up most of the body's tissue) as well as major components of body enzymes and many hormones. Twenty amino acids have been identified for normal growth and tissue formation, although more than twenty exist. Some of these are "essential"; that is, the horse must get them in some form in its diet. The requirements for specific amino acids have not been determined in the horse. However, the normal horse diet appears to supply adequate amounts of all amino acids required.

There is certainly no evidence that would suggest that specific amino acid supplementation is important in horses. Nor have amino acid deficiencies ever been identified as a problem in the horse. While a variety of products containing amino acids are available to give to horses, many of which claim a whole host of beneficial properties, in practice amino acids have little if any therapeutic value.

Just because a horse needs some amino acids doesn't mean that more of them is necessarily better. Excess protein and amino acids are digested by the horse and used for energy; they are an expensive source of energy. In fact, some animal studies have shown that taking unusually large amounts of amino acids can create amino acid imbalances in the animal's body.

AMMONIUM CHLORIDE

Ammonium chloride is a salt that has some pharmaceutical use as an expectorant (see Expectorant).

AMPICILLIN SODIUM   *Amp-Equine*

Ampicillin is an antibiotic used for the treatment of a variety of infections in the horse. It is one of a group of broad-spectrum penicillins, antibiotics that are chemically related to penicillin but that have the ability to kill more kinds of bacteria than does penicillin alone. Ampicillin comes as a dehydrated, sterile powder and is mixed, usually with sterile water, prior to IV or IM injection. The drug can also be infused into the uterus of the mare to treat infections there.

Ampicillin can be used without fear of positive drug tests in horses at AHSA horse shows.

SIDE EFFECTS   Ampicillin has few adverse properties. It should not be used in horses that are allergic to penicillin.

ANABOLIC STEROID

The word "anabolic" refers to building up or constructive processes of cells and tissues. Anabolic steroids are drugs that relate to the sex hormones. Anabolic effects of a drug include improvement of appetite, increased vigor, improvement in musculature and improvement in the hair coat. These drugs may be useful in conditions where there has been marked muscle tissue breakdown, such as with disease, prolonged anorexia or general debilitation from disease or overwork.

Anabolic steroids are also associated with the typical expressions of stallion-like behavior in horses. Horses and mares can show aggressive stallion-like behaviors when given these compounds. In addition, interference with normal estrus cycles is seen in mares maintained on anabolic steroids. Finally, a recent report associates long-term administration of anabolic steroids with dysfunction of the adrenal gland in one horse.

Some people use anabolic steroids to try to enhance performance in horses by trying to build muscle or increase aggressiveness. While the potential to improve performance with these drugs may be there, one study in Scotland failed to show any actual improvement in racehorses treated with these drugs.

Anabolic steroids are closely controlled by the U.S. Food and Drug Administration because of their potential for abuse by humans.

ANTHELCIDE EQ   *(see Benzimidazole)*

35

ANTIBACTERIAL

A substance that destroys bacteria or suppresses their reproduction or growth is an antibacterial.

Antibiotics (see below) have antibacterial effects. Antibacterial compounds used in the treatment of infectious conditions of the horse, such as sulfa drugs, are chemicals that are synthesized in the laboratory. Antibiotics come from naturally occurring microorganisms.

ANTIBIOTIC

An antibiotic is a chemical substance that is produced by a microorganism. This substance has the capacity, when provided in dilute solutions, to inhibit the growth of (bacteriostatic) or to kill (bacteriocidal) other microorganisms. Antibiotics that are sufficiently nontoxic to the host are used in the treatment of many diseases of the horse.

ANTIHISTAMINE

Antihistaminic drugs work to block the effects of histamine in the horse's body. Histamine is a naturally occurring chemical in the horse's body. It seems to have very important effects in the transmission of nerve impulses and in the control of secretions in the stomach.

Histamine is also one of many chemicals that are released during the process of inflammation. It has potent effects on the circulatory system of the horse. In addition to participating in the process of inflammation, histamine is involved in allergic shock (anaphylaxis), allergies and some types of adverse reactions to drugs. Histamine release is associated with swelling of tissue (such as is seen with hives) and itching, among other effects. When skin is scratched, the characteristic resulting redness is due to histamine.

Certain cells have specific locations on them that cause them to respond to histamine. Antihistamines block the effects of histamine by occupying these locations on the cells. Antihistamines do not remove the histamine from the cell sites, however; they only help to prevent further histamine binding to the cell sites.

Antihistamines are useful in countering the effects of histamine in many locations. In horses, they are most commonly used in the treatment of allergic reactions; they help counteract the swelling and itching that are commonly associated with these conditions. Preparations containing antihistamines are sometimes used for treatment of allergic respiratory conditions in horses and for coughing.

Some veterinarians use antihistamine preparations for the treatment of laminitis. The pharmacological basis for this is not clear. Direct infusion of histamine into the horse does not cause laminitis.

Cimetidine and ranitidine are two specific types of histamine-blocking agents used for the treatment and control of gastric ulceration in horses and foals. Cimetidine has also been reported to be effective for treatment of a certain type of equine melanoma, a generally benign skin cancer (see Cimetidine, Ranitidine).

Antihistamine preparations are available in sterile solution for IM administration or in pill form for oral administration in the horse (see Hydroxyzine, Pyrilamine). These drugs are relatively nontoxic at recommended doses.

PRECAUTIONS Antihistamine agents by themselves are frequently ineffective in treating or controlling allergies because many other agents besides histamine are involved in allergic reactions. Antihistamines only help control the symptoms of histamine-associated diseases. Therefore, to get a cure, therapy must also be aimed at removing the cause of the problem.

ANTISEPTIC

An antiseptic is a product that is used to kill or stop the growth of bacteria. The term is always used to refer to products that are used on living tissue. Most antiseptic agents are used to clean the skin of the horse.

ARNICA

Arnica is an herb derived from one of a variety of plants of the genus *Arnica*. In herbal medicine, a tincture of the dried flowers is sometimes applied externally in an effort to help reduce pain and inflammation resulting from bruises and sprains.

Arnica is included as a component of a coolant gel sold over the counter for application to horse limbs (see Coolant Gel). Its effectiveness in horses is unknown.

ARQUEL   (see *Meclofenamic Acid*)

ASPIRIN

Aspirin was introduced in 1899 and is one of the oldest pain relievers used in medicine. Its effects are quite mild. It can be used as a reliever of mild to moderate pain, primarily of muscular or skeletal pain (such as arthritis), and as an agent to control or reduce fever.

Aspirin also tends to inhibit the aggregation (collecting together) of platelets, the cells in the blood that start the first stages of blood clotting. That's why people say that aspirin "thins the blood." Because of this effect on the blood platelets, the use of aspirin is advocated by some veterinarians as an aid in the treatment of laminitis. In laminitis, aspirin is used in an effort to help prevent the formation of blood clots in the circulatory system of the hoof. Aspirin is also advocated by some veterinary ophthalmologists as a good choice for relief of inflammation of the eye.

Aspirin tablets, boluses or powder are available for oral administration in the horse. It is fairly inexpensive.

PRECAUTIONS   Horses with known liver or kidney damage should be monitored closely if on aspirin. Aspirin should not be used in conjunction with aminoglycoside antibiotics (e.g., gentamycin sulfate or amikacin sulfate) because it increases the potential for these drugs to have toxic effects on the kidneys. Caution should be used in giving aspirin to weak, anemic, dehydrated or debilitated animals. It is also recommended that aspirin not be given to animals for two weeks prior to surgery so that blood clotting is not affected. Animals under thirty days of age have difficulty in metabolizing and eliminating aspirin.

SIDE EFFECTS   Aspirin has the potential to cause gastrointestinal ulceration, particularly in large doses. The drug should not be used in horses with ulcers.

ASTRINGENT

Astringent means "causing contraction." Astringent agents are generally applied to the skin. An astringent agent dries and tightens the skin.

In horses, astringents are applied to the skin surface. The effects of an astringent are limited to the skin and they have no effect on the underlying tissues. Astringents work by causing the surface proteins, which are normally in solution, to settle down into solid particles (this process is called precipitation). This can cause the tissue to contract, wrinkle and harden. In high concentrations, astringent substances can be very irritating to the skin.

Therapeutically, astringents can be used to stop bleeding and reduce inflamed mucous membranes. They may have some effect in promoting wound healing, presumably through antiseptic effects (see Antiseptic).

ATROPINE

Atropine is a drug that has a variety of effects on the nervous system of the horse. Although it is frequently used in other species, atropine is rarely used in the horse.

Atropine ointment is most commonly used in treatment of eye inflammation in horses. Atropine causes the eye muscles to relax and dilate, which helps relieve the pain and spasm associated with eye inflammation.

Atropine injections have been used by some veterinarians for treatment of toxicities from organophosphate compounds. It is also an old treatment for colic, since atropine stops intestinal cramping by stopping intestinal movement. However, when atropine is used for treatment of these conditions in horses, it may shut down the movement of the intestines, with potentially fatal consequences. In fact, atropine injections to *healthy* horses can cause the intestines to completely shut down.

· B ·

BACITRACIN *Neosporin, Triple Antibiotic Ointment, Neobacimyx*

Bacitracin is an antibiotic that is available in ointment formulations for applications to wound surfaces or to the surface of the eye. Bacitracin cannot be given systematically because it is toxic.

Bacitracin is almost always combined with two other antibiotics, neomycin and polymixin B (see Neomycin and Polymixin B). This combination increases the numbers of bacteria killed when compared with each antibiotic individually. The rate of wound healing has been shown to increase in wounds treated with this combination of antibiotics. Bacitracin, along with other antibiotics, is also frequently mixed with corticosteroid anti-inflammatory agents (see Corticosteroid).

BACTERIAL SUPPLEMENTS

A number of different bacteria are normally found in the intestinal tract in horses. Some species of intestinal bacteria (such as *E. coli*), while normally present in the intestine, have also been associated with disease states. Other types of intestinal bacteria have not yet been associated with disease and are therefore presumed to be beneficial. In people, for example, *Lactobacillus* species have gained favor in the "natural" health market as being of benefit in the digestive process, in particular in aiding in the digestion of protein.

A variety of nutritional supplements are available for the horse that contain one or more types of dried or live bacteria, including *Lactobacillus, Streptococcus,* and *Bacillus* species. These bacteria are supposed to help the horse to more efficiently digest his feed and to help provide his intestines with a constant supply of "beneficial" bacteria.

There is absolutely no evidence that feeding bacterial supplements to horses is of any benefit. In fact, there are more questions about bacterial supplements than there are answers. For example, how is it possible for living bacteria to exist in a supplement container for many months? For bacteria to grow, reproduce and survive, they require a relatively constant supply of fresh nutrients that could not be provided in a can. If the bacteria are dried, are they still alive? (Feeding a horse dead bacteria couldn't possibly be of benefit.) How can or do the bacteria survive the perilous journey through the horse's stomach, where the environment is so acidic that relatively few bacteria are able to live there under normal circumstances? These questions need to be answered before supplementation with bacteria will be taken seriously by equine nutritionists. Fortunately, bacterial supplements do not seem to cause the horse any harm.

Most frequently, several bacterial species are combined in supplements. One human "natural healing" source suggests that supplementation with a variety of different bacteria is not advisable. It says that the various bacteria may antagonize each other.

In reality, since it is unlikely that bacterial supplementation is of any benefit or harm, it may all just be a moot, though expensive, point.

BALSAM   (*Balsam of Fir, Balsam of Peru*)

A balsam is a resin. Resins are solid or semisolid substances that ooze forth from plants or from insects feeding on plants.

The active ingredients in balsams are two acids, benzoic and cinnamic. Balsams can be used as local skin irritants and are used in the preparation of some wound dressings in the hope that they will stimulate the growth of surface epithelial cells of the skin. In people, balsams are occasionally used for the treatment of bedsores.

BANAMINE   (*see Flunixin Meglumine*)

BEE POLLEN

Bee pollen is a fine, powderlike material that is produced by flowering plants. Bees gather the stuff to make honey.

Bee pollen contains vitamins B and C, some trace minerals and protein. While these things are needed in the horse diet, routine feeding should supply ample amounts of them for the horse.

In people, bee pollen has been promoted to increase energy level. Studies in people have shown no benefit of bee pollen on athletic performance. In fact, some people may be allergic to the stuff. Dramatic claims of healthful benefits from bee pollen for the horse cannot be substantiated.

BENTONITE

Bentonite is a natural earthen clay. It is used in the manufacture of various hoof preparations. It has no known therapeutic value.

BENZALKONIUM CHLORIDE   *Fungisan*

Benzalkonium chloride is an all-purpose antibacterial agent and a mild astringent (see Antibacterial, Astringent). It is the principal ingredient in a commonly used over-the-counter skin preparation for treatment of skin infections of the horse.

Benzalkonium chloride has no effect against viruses or bacterial spores. Importantly, it is inactivated by soaps, which, unfortunately, are commonly applied to wash the surface of the horse's skin prior to application of this product.

When applied to the skin, benzalkonium chloride tends to form a film over the bacteria living on the surface. The bacteria can remain alive under this film. Tissue debris also inactivates benzalkonium chloride, so it has limited effectiveness in areas where tissue fluids are being secreted or on wounds.

BENZELMIN   *(see Benzimidazole)*

BENZIMIDAZOLE

Many varieties of benzimidazole dewormers are available for control of internal parasites in the horse. There are literally hundreds of variations of this type of product that have been investigated by phar-macologists. Preparations are available for the horse for administra-tion in the feed, by oral paste or in a liquid for nasogastric intubation (stomach tube).

Benzimidazole drugs that are commonly used in the horse include thiabendazole, oxfendazole, mebendazole, oxibendazole and fen-bendazole. All of these drugs act in the same fashion, by interfering with the energy-generating mechanisms of the parasites. The drug kills parasites over a two- to three-day period.

In increased doses, benzimidazoles also kill parasite larvae (as does ivermectin, another deworming agent). Killing the immature larvae before they reach the adult stage in the intestines is of obvious benefit. Thiabendazole at ten times the normal dose for two days, fenbendazole at one and a half times the normal dose for five days and oxfendazole at five times the normal dose once have all demonstrated the ability to kill parasite larvae.

These drugs have an extremely wide margin of safety and have been tested at up to forty times overdose. They are safe for use even in young, sick or debilitated animals. There are no reported adverse effects of benzimidazole parasiticides. Products containing cambendazole are not recommended for use in pregnant mares, according to the manufacturer.

Parasite resistance primarily from one group of intestinal para-sites, the "small" stongyles, has been seen against benzimidazole para-siticides. Rotational programs that include other deworming agents are therefore commonly recommended for optimum control of inter-nal parasites in the horse.

Benzimidazoles have little or no effectiveness against tapeworms, bots or parasites of the horse's skin. Combinations of benzimidazole parasiticides and organophosphate dewormers are available for the control of bots, a parasite of the horse's stomach (see Dewormers).

Benzimidazoles do have some antifungal activity. Consequently, they are used by some veterinarians to make antifungal preparations that are applied to the skin of affected horses.

BENZOCAINE

Benzocaine is a local anesthetic, chemically similar to lidocaine or mepivicaine (see Lidocaine, Mepivacaine). Benzocaine is a common ingredient in ointments sold over the counter and applied to the skin in man. Its anesthetic action helps relieve pain associated with surface ulcers and healing wounds.

PRECAUTIONS   Benzocaine is considered a forbidden substance by most organizations that oversee competitions. Benzocaine is used in the preparation of some coolant gels that are applied to horse limbs (see Coolant Gel). Theoretically, if benzocaine were to be absorbed by the horse's body through an open wound, the horse could test positive on drug tests for forbidden substances.

BENZYL ALCOHOL

Benzyl alcohol is normally applied to the skin of the horse. It can be used to help relieve itching and is mildly effective at controlling the growth of bacteria (see Alcohol). Benzyl alcohol is contained in some over-the-counter wound preparations for the horse.

BETA-CAROTENE

Beta-carotene is the dietary precursor of vitamin A (see Vitamin A).

An injectable preparation of beta-carotene has been promoted as an aid in improving the reproductive efficiency of mares.

BETADINE *(see Povidone-Iodine)*

BETAMETHASONE *BetaVet, Celestone Soluspan*

Betamethasone is a steroidal anti-inflammatory drug. Betamethasone suspension is most commonly used for injection into joints to suppress signs of inflammation associated with acute and chronic arthritis.

PRECAUTIONS When betamethasone is administered into a joint, the joint should be clipped of hair and surgically scrubbed with disinfectant solutions prior to injection to help reduce the opportunity for infection (as with any injection into a joint).

After joint injection, horses should be rested for several days prior to a gradual return to normal use.

Occasional acute inflammation ("joint flare") is seen after injection of steroids into joints, resulting in heat, pain and swelling in the affected area. This effect usually disappears rapidly but must be distinguished from a joint infection, a serious problem.

SIDE EFFECTS Steroidal anti-inflammatory drugs such as betamethasone have been accused of accelerating joint destruction in horses with pre-existing arthritis. In joints, corticosteroids have been demonstrated to decrease the metabolism of cartilage cells. This can, apparently, sometimes result in accelerated deterioration of joint surfaces ("steroid arthropathy"). There is, however, little experimental information regarding the effects of injection of steroidal anti-inflammatory agents such as betamethasone into previously damaged or arthritic joints.

Considerable evidence exists that injection of corticosteroids into normal joints is *not* harmful to the joint surfaces, although cartilage metabolism may be affected for up to sixteen weeks after injection. Some clinicians feel that betamethasone is less likely to produce adverse effects in joints than are other corticosteroids (see Corticosteroid).

BIGELOIL   *(see Liniment)*

BIOTIN

Biotin is a vitamin. It is commonly supplemented in the horse's feed to promote improved hoof quality. Initial investigations done on pigs suggested that supplementation with biotin improved hoof quality in that species. Subsequently, several studies have been done in horses that suggest that biotin can help improve the resiliency and quality of the hoof in some horses.

The hoof grows from the coronary band down to the ground. Biotin is only incorporated into the hoof at the growth level, where the hoof is still live tissue. Therefore, it may be several months before any effect from biotin supplementation is seen in the horse's hoof. Unfortunately, sometimes biotin doesn't seem to help horse's feet at all.

Neither biotin toxicity nor biotin deficiency have been reported in horses.

BISMUTH COMPOUNDS   *(subsalicylate, carbonate, etc.)*

Bismuth compounds are used in commonly used antacids and anti-diarrheal products in people. In horses, very large doses of bismuth compounds would have to be given regularly to have any effect in the treatment of ulcers or diarrhea. Therefore, their use in the horse is limited due to the time, expense and mess involved with treatment.

Bismuth compounds are occassionally used for the treatment of stomach ulcers in people. They must be given frequently, six to ten times a day, to have any effect for the treatment of stomach ulcers in people. As with diarrhea, the need for frequent administration of large volumes of this messy compound limits its use for the treatment of gastrointestinal ulcers in horses.

The dose of bismuth in pastes available over the counter is too small to have any significant effect on the treatment of diarrhea. They are certainly not useful in the treatment of abdominal distress (colic) in the horse.

BLISTER

A blister is an extreme form of a counterirritant preparation (see Counterirritant). When applied to the skin of the horse, these compounds cause tremendous inflammation, swelling and pain.

Blistering is an outdated form of treatment that has been in existence for literally hundreds of years. It is most commonly recommended for "treatment" of tendon and ligament injuries in the horse. Most proponents of blistering assert that by creating the tremendous inflammation in the skin, blood is brought into the area and healing is promoted. In all likelihood, nothing of the sort occurs. Blistering only inflames the skin and should have no effect on the circulation to underlying areas.

What blistering does do is enforce rest in the horse. The legs become so swollen and inflamed that the horse cannot move comfortably until the inflammation has subsided. The use of this sort of "therapy" is condemned by the American Humane Society.

BOLDENONE UNDECYLENATE   *Equipoise*

Boldenone undecylenate is a long-acting injectable anabolic steroid for intramuscular administration in horses. It may improve the general state of weakened horses and helps in correcting weight loss and improving appetite. It should be considered only as an adjunct to therapy for specific disease, surgeries and traumatic injuries. Most horses will respond with one or two treatments.

PRECAUTIONS   This drug is a controlled substance by the U.S. Food and Drug Administration because of its potential for abuse by humans.

SIDE EFFECTS   This drug possesses marked androgenic effects. Androgenic effects are those associated with stallion-like behaviors. Thus, overaggressiveness may be noted in horses given this drug. If these effects occur, they may last for up to six or eight weeks, according to the manufacturer.

Studies in mares given boldenone undecylenate show interference with normal estrus behavior (heat). Normal cycles eventually do resume once the drug is withdrawn; however, it may take several months before normal cycles resume. (See also Anabolic Steroids, Stanozolol.)

BORIC ACID

Boric acid is a very weak germicide that is extremely nonirritating. It is used in some preparations to wash out the eye.

Boric acid is also added to some preparations that are used on the hoof. There seems to be little use for boric acid on the horse's hoof.

BRACE

The term *brace* is a synonym for *liniment* (see Liniment).

BREWER'S YEAST

Brewer's yeast is a source of B-vitamins and protein for horses. Horses obtain all the B-vitamins that they need from their diet and from synthesis of the vitamins by bacteria in the intestines. There are no reports of deficiencies or toxicities of B-vitamins in the horse, nor is

222

there evidence of toxicity caused by supplementation with brewer's yeast. Other, less expensive protein supplements are available should this form of supplementation be desired (see Vitamin B, Protein).

"BUTE" *(see Phenylbutazone)*

BUTORPHANOL *Torbugesic*

Butorphanol is an analgesic (a pain-relieving agent) for the horse. It comes as a sterile solution that is most commonly used intravenously. Butorphanol has been shown to be effective for the relief of pain arising from colic in experimental situations, with relief lasting up to four hours. Butorphanol is not as effective as the drugs xylazine or detomodine at relief of abdominal pain, however. Its sedative effects are not as profound as these drugs, either. To decrease the sedative side effects of xylazine on the horse, butorphanol is usually used in combination with xylazine to provide increased analgesic effects. Clinical experience suggests that this combination of drugs also tends to reduce the horse's reaction to external stimuli when compared with the sedative effects of xylazine alone.

PRECAUTIONS   As with other tranquilizers, care should be used in working around horses that are under the effects of this drug. Horses are still able to react to external stimuli when they are tranquilized. There are no controlled studies on the use of butorphanol in breeding horses, weanlings or foals.

SIDE EFFECTS   Toxic effects of butorphanol are not seen until the dosage is exceeded by twenty times. Mild sedation is seen in some horses following administration. The most commonly seen side effect is mild incoordination or stumbling, which can last for up to ten minutes. Occasionally, this incoordination can be more pronounced.

· C ·

CALCIUM

Calcium is a mineral with many important functions in the horse's body. The most important function is as a structural component of bone. It is also extremely important for normal muscle contraction.

Calcium levels are closely associated with levels of phosphorus, and both minerals are needed for normal bone formation (see Phosphorus). The "balance" between levels of calcium and phosphorus (the calcium to phosphorus ratio) in the horse's diet has been extensively studied. The balance in the diet between calcium and phosphorus is of great concern to many horse owners. As long as the minimum dietary requirements for both calcium and phosphorus are met, however, the balance in the diet of these minerals appears to be somewhat less important than the absolute levels of each mineral.

Calcium levels are largely controlled by vitamin D (see Vitamin D). Control of body calcium levels is very complex. Naturally occurring incidences of excess calcium supplementation have not been reported. Alfalfa hay has high amounts of calcium in it and most horses get adequate amounts of dietary calcium. Calcium-deficient diets have been reported, although rarely. When combined with an excess of phosphorus, calcium deficiency can result in a condition called nutritional secondary hyperparathyroidism, a disease characterized by abnormalities in the bones and lameness. This condition also is extremely rare.

Significant amounts of calcium can be lost in the sweat of exercising horses as well as in the milk of lactating mares, particularly draft horse mares. Additional dietary calcium will not prevent these conditions. In the case of lactating mares, additional dietary calcium prior to giving birth actually tends to make it more likely that there will be a problem with excessive calcium loss in the milk. In the case of exercising horses, calcium loss is associated with interference with normal muscle function. If either of these conditions occur, treatment with calcium-containing solutions must be given at the time they appear.

Calcium supplements or injections of calcium-containing solutions have been advocated by some people as a method of "natural" tranquilization for the horse. There is no medical evidence supporting the use of calcium for this purpose.

CAMPHOR

Camphor is a natural compound obtained by distilling the chips and leaves of the camphor tree. It has a distinct, characteristic odor.

Camphor has several weak pharmacologic properties. It is mildly effective as an antiseptic and an anesthetic (anti-itch) when applied to the skin. Camphor also has some counterirritant properties and is used in a variety of liniments for the horse applied to the leg or body (see Counterirritant, Liniment). Camphor has no effect on inflammation in the underlying tissues over which it is applied.

CAPSICUM

Capsicum is what makes cayenne pepper hot. It contains small amounts of vitamins.

In herbal medicine, capsicum has a variety of uses for things such as nausea, rheumatism and arthritis. Capsicum is also the principal ingredient of a powder that people put in their socks to help their feet feel warm. It is irritating to surface tissue and thus functions as a counterirritant (see Counterirritant). Capsicum is a component of a few of the over-the-counter liniment products that are made for the horse.

CAPTAN

Captan is a rose and plant fungicide that has been occasionally recommended for the treatment of fungal skin infections of the horse. Clinical experience with captan has shown it to be largely ineffective in treatment of these conditions. If chosen for skin therapy, captan should be used with care. The drug commonly causes skin allergies and sensitivities in people. Captan is also being investigated as a potential cancer-causing agent.

CARAFATE   (see Sucralfate)

CARBOCAINE   (see Mepivacaine)

CASTOR OIL

Castor oil is obtained from the seed of the castor bean plant. Its existence dates from the time of the ancient Egyptians. In man, castor oil can be used externally or internally. Internally, it acts as a cathartic and is used to empty the gastrointestinal tract. Externally, castor oil is used as an emollient (see Emollients). In the horse, castor oil is most commonly used externally and is a common component of various hoof dressings, presumably for its emollient properties (see Hoof Dressings.) Given internally, castor oil can cause severe diarrhea in horses.

CATAPLASM

The term *cataplasm* is a synonym for *poultice* (see Poultice).

CEDARWOOD OIL   *(see Pine Oil)*

CEFTIOFUR SODIUM   *Naxcel*

Ceftiofur sodium is a relatively new antibiotic for use in the horse. Ceftiofur is the only member of the cephalosporin group of antibiotics that is approved for use in horses. Other members of this group of antibiotics have wide usage in both human and veterinary medicine because they kill many different bacteria with few adverse effects.

Ceftiofur comes as a sterile powder. It is mixed with sterile water prior to administration by intramuscular injection. It is also given IV by some veterinarians.

SIDE EFFECTS   Ceftiofur appears to be relatively safe for use in the horse. Occasional reports of diarrhea and colitis have been mentioned as potential side effects.

CETYL ALCOHOL

Cetyl alcohol is an ointment base that has wide use in the manufacture of cosmetic creams and lotions. It helps ointments retain their consistency. Cetyl alcohol makes human skin feel smooth. Cetyl alcohol is a component of various hoof dressings (see Hoof Dressings).

CHARCOAL

Charcoal is almost pure carbon, the residue of burning wood in the air. Charcoal is generally treated by a number of chemical processes to increase its ability to adsorb (attract and retain material on the surface) substances. This process is referred to as activation. Activated charcoal is most commonly given orally, to help adsorb toxins after poisonings. Charcoal has no recognized value in the treatment of diarrhea, although it has been used for that. Charcoal is also available in an over-the-counter wound preparation for horses; there are no known benefits from charcoal in treating wounds.

CHELATED MINERALS

Some minerals are metallic elements, such as zinc, iron or magnesium. To chelate means to bind a metal element to another substance. In the case of minerals, they are often bound to amino acids, the building blocks of proteins.

Manufacturers claim that chelated minerals are absorbed more quickly by the body than are nonchelated minerals. In fact, chelated minerals are rapidly separated from the amino acids in the stomach and intestines and are then absorbed just like nonchelated minerals. There is certainly no evidence that shows that chelated minerals are absorbed any better than nonchelated minerals. Most horses don't need mineral supplementation anyway (see Mineral).

CHLORAMPHENICOL

Chloramphenicol is an antibiotic that is rarely used in horses but can be effective for certain infectious conditions. In horses, it is most commonly given orally and is available in pill or capsule form. It is also available as a preparation to put in the eye to help treat infected eye injuries (ulcers).

Chloramphenicol is a unique drug because it has a tremendous ability to penetrate areas of the body that are not readily penetrated by other drugs, such as the chest cavity, the eye and the spinal canal. Unfortunately, for it to be effective when given orally, it has to be administered four times a day.

PRECAUTIONS   In man, chloramphenicol is rarely used because it can cause the body to stop producing red blood cells (aplastic anemia). Aplastic anemia has not been seen in animals receiving chloramphenicol. This bad effect is not related to the dose of the drug. Any amount of chloramphenicol, even if it is just by exposure to the skin, can be dangerous to people who are susceptible to this effect. It has been estimated that between 1 in 40,000 to 1 in 200,000 people may be adversely affected by chloramphenicol. Because of this bad effect on people, the use of chloramphenicol is prohibited in animals intended for food.

Thus, chloramphenicol should be handled carefully. Latex gloves should be worn while handling the drug and care should be taken not to breathe dust from the drug or to get it in your mouth. Many people choose to wear protective face masks while giving the drug. It is quite bitter and horses do not eat it readily, so it usually has to be given with a balling gun or dosing syringe. That can be quite messy.

Chloramphenicol does have an effect on the enzymes of the liver. It can delay the metabolism of certain substances by the liver. Therefore, it should be employed with caution when other drugs that are processed by the liver, such as some anesthetic or anticonvulsant agents, are used.

Chloramphenicol should not be administered prior to giving barbiturate anesthetic agents (which are commonly used to begin anesthesia in the horse). It is also recommended that the simultaneous use of chloramphenicol and immunizing agents (vaccines) be avoided.

SIDE EFFECTS   Adverse reactions to chloramphenicol do not occur very often. In practically all respects, the drug is free of bad effects on the gastrointestinal and nervous systems. It does not seem to be associated with allergic reactions, either.

Chloramphenicol should not be used with penicillin-type drugs. Penicillins work only on growing bacteria and chloramphenicol interferes with the growth of bacteria (it does not kill them directly).

CHLORHEXIDINE   *Nolvasan, Chlorhexiderm, Chlorasan, Virosan, Solvahex*

Chlorhexidine is a disinfectant and antiseptic. Its uses are similar to povidone-iodine (see Povidone-Iodine). When compared with povidone-iodine, cleansing the skin with chlorhexidine causes a more immediate reduction in surface bacteria and has a longer residual action. However, experimentally chlorhexidine has been shown to slow wound healing if it is not completely rinsed from a wound in which it was used as a cleaning agent. It comes as a solution and as a solution-containing soap; there is also a chlorhexidine ointment available for the treatment of wounds of the horse.

CHLOROXYLENOL

Chloroxylenol is a derivative of coal tar oil. Chloroxylenol and related products are primarily used to preserve wood. Chloroxylenol is found in a commonly used liniment for the horse (see Liniment). It is of no known therapeutic value.

CHONDROITIN SULFATE   *Cosequin, Flex-Free, etc.*

Chondroitin sulfate is an oral supplement for the horse. It is most commonly recommended for treatment of arthritis and conditions involving joints.

Chondroitin sulfate is one of a variety of substances, called glycosaminoglycans, that are found in normal horse joints. They are structural components of joint cartilage and connective tissues and they help form the matrix that exists around cartilage cells. When they are supplemented in the feed, chondroitin sulfates have been demonstrated to appear in the joints of rats.

Whether this makes any difference in the horse is another question. No controlled studies have been performed on the horse to show what, if any, benefit can be obtained from chondroitin sulfate supplementation. It is not known if the product is absorbed by the horse's intestines. There is no evidence at this time to indicate that supplementation of these products has any protective effect on joint cartilage, any anti-inflammatory effect or any lubricant effect in arthritic joints in the horse. Reports of beneficial effects are not supported by scientific studies at this point in time. No side effects have been reported from the use of chondroitin sulfate products in the horse.

The use and effects of chondroitin sulfate supplementation in horses is under study by the veterinary community. If it is effective, chondroitin sulfate should act in the same manner as polysulfated glycosaminoglycan (see Polysulfated glycosaminogycan). Indeed, some veterinarians have reported beneficial effects in the treatment of arthritis with these products. No adverse side effects have been reported from the use of chondroitin sulfate products in the horse.

CIMETIDINE *Tagamet*

Cimetidine is a specific type of histamine antagonist (antihistamine) that is occasionally used in the horse for the treatment of stomach ulcers. It has also been reported useful for the treatment of a specific type of melanoma (a type of skin cancer) in the horse.

Cimetidine is supplied as a tablet for oral administration in the horse. The drug is quite safe and is effective for the treatment of stomach ulcers, although a newer drug, ranitidine, has come to be favored for treatment of this condition by some veterinarians.

No significant side effects have been reported from the use of cimetidine in horses.

CLIOQUINOL   *Rheaform*

Clioquinol is occasionally recommended for treatment of diarrhea in the horse. It is an anti-protozoal agent. Clioquinol is available as a large pill (bolus) for oral administration to the horse.

It is not known why clioquinol helps horses with diarrhea. (Its effect does not appear to be related to its ability to kill protozoa.) Many horses that respond to clioquinol therapy will resume diarrhea once treatment is stopped.

COCONUT OIL

Coconut oil is obtained by pressing coconuts seeds. It has no known pharmaceutical properties but it smells like coconut. It is a component of a variety of hoof dressings for the horse (see Hoof Dressings), possibly because it smells good.

COD LIVER OIL

Cod liver oil comes from steam-cooking the liver of the codfish. Cod liver oil is made up primarily of oils but it also contains high levels of vitamins A and D and iodine. In people, it is used primarily as a vitamin supplement. In horses, cod liver oil is a component of some hoof dressings, presumably because it contains vitamins and oils. Cod liver oil is not used externally in people. What effect cod liver oil would have on horse hoof is unknown, although because it is an oil it may have some emollient effects (see Emollients, Hoof Dressings). It is not possible for the dead hoof tissue to absorb the vitamins found in cod liver oil.

COOLANT GEL

Many attractively colored gels are available to put on the legs of the horse. These are usually sold over the counter and are purported to provide a cooling and anti-inflammatory effect on the limbs. They are generally used to treat what are perceived by the owner to be minor swellings or strains of the various joints, ligaments or tendons.

Coolant gels generally contain one or more of the following ingredients: menthol, camphor, thymol, witch hazel, eucalyptus oil, magnesium sulfate or other salts and various alcohols (see various headings). In man, such ingredients are commonly used as mild counterirritants and antiseptics. They have a very pleasant, volatile smell and they evaporate quickly. Evaporation of substances from the skin gives a cooling sensation. What, if any, effect coolant gels have on underlying tissues is unknown, at best. These products are certainly not therapeutic for more severe injuries.

Some coolant gel products contain benzocaine, a local anesthetic agent (see Benzocaine). Care should be taken in using these products so as to avoid causing the horse to test positively on drug tests in competition.

COPPER

Copper is a trace mineral that is an essential part of many of the systems of the horse's body. Copper is involved in blood production, bone production and skin pigmentation, to name but a few of its functions. Copper is also important for normal function of some of the enzyme systems of the horse's body. Relationships exist between levels of copper and zinc, as well as levels of copper and molybdenum. Copper is also important for the normal absorption of iron.

Most horse diets have adequate levels of copper and copper deficiencies are virtually unheard of in adult horses. However, it has been suggested by some researchers that increasing levels of dietary copper in young horses may be useful in helping to prevent the occurrence of osteochondrosis, a disease that results in abnormal cartilage development in growing foals.

COPPER NAPTHENATE   *Kopertox*

Copper napthenate is the main ingredient in a number of preparations for the treatment of thrush, an infectious condition of the horse's hoof. It is a caustic chemical that dries the hoof tissue and destroys the infectious agents. It appears to be an effective treatment for controlling thrush.

COPPER SULFATE

Copper sulfate is a chemical found in a number of preparations sold over the counter for wound treatment in the horse. Copper sulfate is a caustic chemical. It causes local tissue destruction. As a wound treatment, copper sulfate causes a hard scab to form on tissue. It causes surface proteins to come out of solution (to "precipitate").

Copper sulfate does kill bacteria directly, but the formation of a chemical scab on healing tissue is not necessarily a good thing. In fact, the growth of bacteria may even be favored underneath the protection of the chemically caused scab. The treatment of wounds with harsh caustic substances is generally not recommended. The rationale for inducing a chemical burn onto healing tissue is difficult to understand.

CORTICOSTEROID

Corticosteroids are a large group of hormones that are produced by the adrenal gland, a small gland that lies next to the kidneys of the horse. These hormones have many extremely important functions in the horse's body.

Various synthetic hormones have been made in an attempt to help reproduce the beneficial effects of corticosteroids. These drugs are a part of medical therapy for many conditions. The most important effects of the corticosteroids in medicine are anti-inflammatory. Used correctly, corticosteroids are safe and effective agents for reducing inflammation of a variety of tissues and are very useful in combatting allergic reactions. Various corticosteroid preparations are given intravenously, in the muscle, orally, into joints and on the surface of the body, as well as both on and in the eye. The drugs are also used in the treatment of early stages of shock. Animals that receive corticosteroid therapy seem to feel better immediately.

Many types of corticosteroid exist (see Betamethasone, Dexamethasone, Prednisone/Prednisolone, Triamcinolone). There are differences in potency and duration of action among the various agents, but selection of various corticosteroid drugs is largely a matter of the experience of the veterinarian and the cost of the drug.

It is important to realize that corticosteroids are not a cure for any disease process. Their anti-inflammatory effects can quiet a variety of inflammatory conditions and this is certainly useful, but relief is frequently only temporary. In the treatment of conditions such as arthritis, for example, corticosteroids can help alleviate inflammation of the joint. However, the arthritis is not cured by the treatment. Similarly, corticosteroids can control the abnormal responses seen with allergic reactions ("hives") but they do not desensitize the horse to whatever it is that he is allergic to.

PRECAUTIONS   Corticosteroid drugs should be used very carefully in the face of infection. While corticosteroid products are good agents for the relief of inflammation, inflammation is an important and necessary response of the body to help combat infection. If the inflammatory response is suppressed, infections may be able to spread more easily. Similarly, while corticosteroid agents suppress the immune system when it's out of control (that's why, for example, they help control allergies), this effect is not at all good when the body is trying to fight off an infection. The body needs a fully functioning immune system to help combat disease-producing agents. For the same reasons, corticosteroids should not be given at the same time as vaccines, so as to avoid impeding the normal immune response to vaccination.

Corticosteroid preparations should never be used to treat an eye that has an ulcer in it. Ulcers are disruptions in the surface of the cornea (the covering of the eye) that most commonly occur from trauma to the eye. Corticosteroids retard or prevent healing on the ulcerated surface of the eye.

Corticosteroid ointments can be applied to skin wounds to help control the growth of granulation tissue (see Wound Treatments). A few days after the occurrence of a wound on the skin, corticosteroid ointments applied to the wound surface have no adverse effect on healing.

Caution should be used in giving corticosteroids to mares that are late in their pregnancies. The drug has the potential to induce labor in later-term mares. Mares early in gestation do not abort their fetuses when given corticosteroids, however.

SIDE EFFECTS It is generally accepted in medicine that to prevent negative effects of corticosteroids, the drugs should be used at the lowest effective dose possible for the shortest period of time necessary. In the body, naturally occurring levels of corticosteroids are carefully controlled by a complex mechanism. Corticosteroids are synthetic drugs that mimic the effects of the naturally occurring substances. If the drugs are administered regularly and in high enough doses, the body may not feel the need to produce its own corticosteroids, relying instead on the drug from the outside. This is loosely referred to as drug dependence. Once the drug is removed, then, the body may not be ready to produce the required "natural" amounts of the hormone. This can cause serious health problems. For this reason, it is commonly recommended in most species that corticosteroids be withdrawn from the body slowly, with a decreasing dosage over a period of time.

Prolonged corticosteroid therapy in dogs or man also commonly produces a whole host of other side effects, such as weight gain, increased appetite, increased thirst, increased urination, gastrointestinal ulceration and tissue wasting. For some reason, however, horses seem to be particularly insensitive to the negative effects of corticosteroids and of drug dependence. Horses seem to tolerate relatively large doses of these drugs for prolonged periods of time with few adverse side effects and little need for slow withdrawal. Many veterinarians prefer, however, to slowly withdraw horses from corticosteroid therapy just in case negative effects might be seen.

In horses, two significant side effects of corticosteroid drugs are reported. Laminitis ("founder") is a serious condition affecting the hoof of the horse. The use of corticosteroid drugs has occasionally been associated with the onset of laminitis. This is certainly not a common side effect and the reasons for its occurrence are poorly understood. High doses and prolonged use of longer-acting systemic corticosteroid products are more likely to produce laminitis than the judicious use of these agents. It is generally accepted that corticosteroids should not be used in the treatment of laminitis.

Steroidal anti-inflammatory drugs have been accused of accelerating joint destruction in horses, especially those that have pre-existing arthritis. Some people accept this as fact. The medical studies are far from clear on this, however. Corticosteroids have the effect of impeding normal tissue metabolism. In a joint, this effect would tend to retard or prevent the normal processes, including the process of repair of damaged tissue. Theoretically, then, if the joint is prevented from repairing itself, destruction of the joint can continue without interference, leading to the so-called steroid arthropathy.

While steroid arthropathies have been described, in reality their occurrence is not very common. Certainly the negative side effects of corticosteroid injections should be considered if they are to be given into arthritic joints. However, not all joints injected with corticosteroids will develop steroid arthropathies and many arthritic joints benefit from the relief of inflammation, even if only temporarily. There is, however, little experimental information regarding the effects of injection of corticosteroidal anti-inflammatory agents into previously damaged or arthritic joints. Considerable evidence exists that injection of steroids into normal joints is not harmful. The actual effects of corticosteroid injection into joints is the cause of much discussion in the veterinary community.

CORTISONE

Cortisone is a generic term that is used to describe a variety of drugs referred to as corticosteroids (see Corticosteroid). There is no drug used in the horse by the name of *cortisone*.

COUNTERIRRITANT

A counterirritant is a substance that, when applied to the surface of the skin, produces mild irritation and inflammation. Counterirritant effects are caused primarily by local blood vessel dilation, which, in man, produces a sensation of heat, comfort and sometimes itching. When the irritation is severe, these agents cause damage to surface capillaries. Plasma leaking from damaged capillaries results in the formation of blisters (see Blister).

The concept of counterirritation is very old, probably even prehistoric. Hundreds of years ago, it was thought that inflammation could not exist in two places at one time. As a result, counterirritation was developed as a method of inciting inflammation in one area so as to relieve it in another. This concept, of course, is not true; inflammation can exist simultaneously in many areas.

In man, counterirritants are commonly applied to the skin to help relieve muscle soreness and stiffness. The sensation of heat produced by the irritation caused by these agents does seem to help relieve minor stiffness and soreness in some cases. The reason for this effect is poorly understood.

Many counterirritant products are available for use in the horse. Whether horses have the same response to counterirritant therapy as do humans is pure speculation. What, if any, effect they have in the horse is unknown. This fact has not, of course, limited their use.

CREOSOTE

Creosote is a mixture of volatile chemicals (phenols) that is obtained from wood tar. One of its main components is guaiacol (see Guaiacol).

Creosote has very weak antiseptic properties. It has been used in steam inhalers as an expectorant. It is also occasionally used as a disinfectant.

Creosote was previously also used as a wood preservative. As such, it has been used to paint fences to keep horses from eating them, since it has a bitter taste. Creosote, however, is very toxic. Horses eating creosote-treated wood can conceivably be poisoned, so it is now largely unavailable as a wood preservative.

Creosote is a component of an over-the-counter poultice for use in horses, possibly because it is a disinfectant. There are no other known medicinal properties of creosote that would explain why it would be included in such a preparation.

CRESOL

Cresol is obtained from coal tar or crude oil. It is similar to phenol in its medicinal qualities (see Phenol). Cresol has disinfectant and antiseptic properties but it is of very low potency. It is sometimes used to wash floors. Cresol is a component of an over-the-counter hoof dressing (see Hoof Dressings).

CRYSTAL VIOLET *Blue Lotion*

Crystal violet is a dye that is used in the treatment of surface wounds of the horse. It kills surface bacteria when applied to the skin. Although crystal violet is effective at killing bacteria, it is not frequently used because it stains clothes and turns the horse purple where it is applied. Crystal violet has also been used to treat burns in people.

· D ·

DETOMODINE *Dormosedan*

Detomodine is a sedative and analgesic agent. It is from the same class of drugs as xylazine (see Xylazine). Detomodine comes as a sterile solution for IM or IV injection.

When compared to xylazine, the sedative effects of detomodine are two to three times as long-lasting, depending on the dose. It also produces a deeper, more profound sedation than does xylazine. Horses usually stand very still, with their heads low to the ground, after they have received an injection of detomodine. These qualities can be useful during minor surgical procedures, where redosing of drugs may be inconvenient or impractical.

As an analgesic, detomodine is extremely effective for the control of abdominal pain (colic). The length of time that pain relief lasts also depends on the dose. Detomodine appears to be able to control most types of severe colic pain. Because of this, it may mask pain signs that would indicate that a colic requires surgery to correct the problem. A thorough evaluation of the horse is imperative while pain control with detomodine is maintained.

Detomodine is safe at five to ten times normal doses.

PRECAUTIONS   Detomodine should not be used in horses with abnormal heart rhythms, heart insufficiencies, respiratory disease or chronic kidney failure. The effects of detomodine on breeding horses and fetuses have not been studied.

Caution should always be used when working around any sedated horse. Even though deeply sedated, some horses may still respond to external stimuli. Routine safety precautions should always be used around horses sedated with detomodine or any other drug.

Detomodine use is forbidden in show horses by the AHSA. After administration of detomodine, drug residues can be detected for up to sixty days. The test does not identify levels of the drug, only its presence.

SIDE EFFECTS   After dosage with detomodine, it is common to observe a heart rhythm abnormality known as second degree A-V block. This is best described as the heart having a pattern of regularly slowing down and then skipping a beat. This is apparently not dangerous for the horse.

Sweating is also common after administration of detomodine. This is an effect of the drug on sweat glands and is not a sign of an abnormal or dangerous response.

Detomodine causes a long-term sedation that is most obviously manifested by the horse lowering his head. Sometimes swelling or passive congestion of the gums, lips or facial area may be seen if the horse's head stays down for a period of time (from the fact that the circulatory system has difficulty building up enough pressure to get all the fluid out of the lowered head). Mucus discharges from the nose may be seen as well. These effects are not serious and may be relieved by elevating the head.

Urination usually occurs after recovery from detomodine sedation, usually at about forty-five to sixty minutes after injection.

DEWORMERS

Many agents exist for the control of intestinal parasites in the horse. They come in one of three formulations: oral paste, liquid for administration by nasogastric tube (stomach tube) and powdered or pelleted for application in or on the feed.

Dozens of studies have shown that all of the above formulations appear to be equally effective in controlling intestinal parasites, assuming that: (1) the horse is given the proper dose for his weight and (2) the horse gets the whole dose. A recent comparison showed that even if some wastage or loss occurs when oral pastes are given, this is probably not enough to be significant.

Occasional nasogastric intubation ("tube worming") is not necessary for control of internal parasites in the horse. While the stomach tube does deliver all of the medication into the horse's stomach or lower esophagus, this offers no particular advantage over oral pastes or feed-based pellets. Also, the formulations that are delivered via a tube are of no greater potency than other formulations.

Deworming products are generally quite safe and have a wide margin of safety. Most drugs have been tested at up to forty times normal dose with few adverse effects. The singular exception to this are products that contain organophosphate chemicals such as trichlorfon. Organophosphates have occasionally been reported to cause adverse effects such as staggering or seizure at normal doses, and are not safe at twice normal doses. Occasional allergic reactions have also been reported to deworming products, especially ivermectin.

For additional information on individual deworming products, see various specific headings (Ivermectin, Febantel, Benzimidazole, Pyrantel, Trichlorfon, Piperazine).

DEXAMETHASONE   *Azium, Dexameth-a-Vet, Dexasone*

Dexamethasone is a corticosteroid product for the control of inflammation in the horse. It is available as a sterile solution for intramuscular or intravenous injection and as a powder for oral administration.

Two types of solutions of dexamethasone are available for use. Dexamethasone sodium phosphate is considered a rapid-onset corticosteroid. Dexamethasone acetate is considered to have a longer duration of action. These differences are due to the chemical configuration of the different products.

Some people feel that dexamethasone has a calming effect on horses. As such, it is occasionally used in an attempt to quiet horses prior to competitions. There is no medical evidence that the drug is effective when used in this way. The potential side effects of repeated doses of dexamethasone should also be considered before using the drug in this manner.

PRECAUTIONS AND SIDE EFFECTS   Dexamethasone should be used with the same precautions and has the same side effects as any of the corticosteroid agents (see Corticosteroid).

DEXTROSE

Dextrose is sugar and sugar provides energy. Dextrose is available as a sterile solution for intravenous administration. It is also commonly added to electrolyte supplements for oral administration in the horse.

As a practical matter, dextrose administration is rarely required for treatment of any condition of the normal horse. Dextrose solutions are probably best employed when horses are not eating normally, due to disease processes, for example. The solutions are also useful in the treatment of shock. In horses that are weak and debilitated, dextrose solutions alone are not able to meet all of the metabolic needs of the horse.

Foals do not have the same metabolic reserves as adult horses; that is, they are not very big and they have very little fat. Consequently, dextrose solutions are commonly used to help maintain energy levels in sick foals.

The oral dextrose that is provided in electrolyte preparations is in insufficient amounts to have any significant effect at the recommended dosages.

PRECAUTIONS   Overuse of dextrose solutions can increase dehydration by causing water to be excreted by the kidneys. Too much sugar in the blood has to be removed from the system. That job is the responsibility of kidneys. In the process, water, as well as sodium, is lost by the horse's body.

SIDE EFFECTS   There are no reported adverse side effects for dextrose at normal doses.

DIAZEPAM   *Valium*

Diazepam is a sedative agent that is rarely used in the horse. It comes as a sterile solution for intramuscular or intravenous injection.

Diazepam has little use in the horse on its own because the effects of the drug are not profound and the quality of sedation that is produced is not desirable for minor surgical procedures or other situations where sedation is desired. However, the use of diazepam to try to calm competitive show horses has been alleged. The drug is easily detectable and its use is forbidden by the AHSA.

Diazepam has been used in combination with ketamine and xylazine in the horse to help smooth induction and recovery during general anesthesia. Here, the drug is used for its muscle relaxant properties.

DIMETHYLGLYCINE   *(DMG)*

DMG is a dietary supplement. The substance is present in many foods. It is supposed to increase the utilization of oxygen and decrease the production of lactic acid by the muscles during high-intensity exercise.

Several studies on DMG in people have shown that it does not have any consistent effects. The studies that have been done on DMG in horses have shown conflicting results. One study has suggested that DMG may reduce lactic acid levels in exercising horses. However, another, more recent, study concluded that exercising horses given DMG had no improvement in oxygen carrying by the blood. Nor was there any change in lactic acid concentration in the plasma, blood or muscle in this study.

In man, DMG has also been advocated to help improve the immune response to viral agents. This effect has not been demonstrated in horses.

In horses, DMG has most commonly been promoted as a substance to help reduce the incidence of acute or chronic equine exertional rhabdomyolysis, also known as "tying up," myositis or azoturia. There is no scientific evidence to suggest that DMG actually would do this. Furthermore, the mechanism by which it would exert its effect is somewhat unclear, as lactic acid production (as measured in the blood) does not appear to be a feature of rhabdomyolysis in the horse.

DIMETHYL SULFOXIDE (DMSO) Domoso

One of the most frequently employed and interesting substances with which to treat horses is a chemical solvent containing a variety of unique and interesting properties. It has been credited with over thirty properties for the treatment of disease and is therefore used in a wide variety of applications in the horse. This substance goes by the name of dimethyl sulfoxide, abbreviated to DMSO.

DMSO is available in a gel or in a liquid form. The liquid form can be given orally, intravenously (when diluted) or applied on top of the skin; the gel is always used topically. The use of the drug is generally based on the veterinarian's experience and reading. Fortunately, DMSO is a fairly benign substance. As frequently as it is used, surprisingly little study has gone into its application in horses.

As a therapeutic agent, DMSO is used primarily as an anti-inflammatory. There are a variety of ways that DMSO exerts its effect as an anti-inflammatory, of which the most important seems to be the neutralization of some of the destructive substances that are produced by the process of inflammation. In addition to this, DMSO has some of the same anti-inflammatory properties as do the corticosteroids. DMSO can be used at the same time as these drugs. DMSO will even help protect tissues from injury induced by a lack of blood (called ischemia; you can make your finger ischemic by putting a tight rubber band around it, for example). There are a variety of other useful properties of DMSO, too. Because DMSO has such a wide array of alluring medical possibilities for treatment, it is used quite a bit in veterinary medicine.

DMSO is unique in that it can go through the skin and mucous membranes without disrupting them. Because of this property, it can be used as a carrier of other substances through the skin. When DMSO is mixed with corticosteroids, for instance, the level of the corticosteroids in the tissue is increased by a factor of three! And because it can go through the skin, people who use DMSO report tasting it after they put it on (or in) their horse.

DMSO is very volatile. When it is absorbed through the skin, it rapidly enters the circulatory system. The DMSO travels around until it reaches the lungs, at which point it exits the system and gets breathed out. Of course, the air that is breathed out comes up the back of your mouth and that is why it can be tasted. People report that DMSO tastes like onions or garlic; although the taste may be unpleasant, it certainly isn't harmful.

The wide variety of conditions that DMSO is used to treat almost defies belief. There are reports of using the stuff topically to treat swellings; injecting it into joints; using it systemically for muscle soreness, disease of the nervous system and treatment of colic and its associated effects; in the reproductive tract of the mare; for skin conditions; to accelerate wound healing; to prevent blood clotting and for laminitis, to name but a few. Because of its ability to penetrate membranes, DMSO is also commonly employed to help get drugs into areas that are hard to reach, like the brain or the chest cavity. So if it seems that DMSO is being used to treat almost everything, it's because it probably is.

There are no standard doses that have been generated for DMSO. For most drugs, dose ranges based on half-lives and desired blood levels have been established. With DMSO this is not the case. Furthermore, most of the things that DMSO is used for are outside those uses recommended by the manufacturer. Finally, in the treatment of most medical conditions for which it is used in the horse, no controlled studies have been done to establish how well the stuff works in treating the conditions.

Fortunately, considering how widely it is used, DMSO is pretty benign and has a very low toxicity. It is so safe that it can be drunk and it can also be given intravenously (it should be diluted first).

DINOPROST   *(see Prostaglandins and the Reproductive Cycle of the Mare)*

DIOCTYL SODIUM SULFOSUCCINATE   *(DSS)*

Dioctyl sodium sulfosuccinate (DSS) is used for the treatment of colic. It acts to reduce surface tension in the fecal mass. By doing so, DSS allows water to more easily penetrate masses of fecal matter. In addition, DSS causes the intestine to secrete fluid and electrolytes. As such, it can function as a stool softener and laxative. DSS is a liquid that is diluted with water and given by nasogastric intubation.

DSS can also be diluted with water and given in an enema to foals for treatment of retained meconium. (Meconium is the first fecal material the foal passes.)

PRECAUTIONS   DSS should not be given at the same time as mineral oil. DSS has the potential to break down mineral oil into small enough globules that it can be absorbed into the circulation.

SIDE EFFECTS   DSS has the potential to be irritating to the intestinal tract. Overdosage of DSS can create diarrhea and make horses feel quite sick. Recommended doses of DSS should be repeated only every forty-eight hours.

DIPYRONE

Dipyrone is a mild anti-inflammatory and analgesic for the horse. It can also be used to help control fevers. Dipyrone is chemically related to phenylbutazone and works in the same fashion. Dipyrone is supplied as a sterile solution for IM, IV or subcutaneous administration.

Dipyrone is most commonly used for the control of abdominal pain (colic) in the horse. Experiments show that the drug is certainly not very potent. Some people even believe that it has no value in the control of colic pain.

PRECAUTIONS   If dipyrone is given for a prolonged period, problems with decreased white blood cells may be seen. The drug should not be used at the same time as barbiturate agents (commonly used to induce anesthesia in the horse). Racehorses should not be given dipyrone for five days before a race because it is considered a masking agent.

If given in the vein, dipyrone should be given very slowly to avoid convulsions. It should be used with care in horses with heart disease.

SIDE EFFECTS   Side effects of dipyrone are similar to those of aspirin (see Aspirin). Overdosage of dipyrone can cause seizures.

DISINFECTANT

A disinfectant is an agent that kills disease-causing microorganisms. The term is properly used when referring to killing microorganisms on inanimate objects, such as surgical instruments or stalls.

DORMOSEDAN   *(see Detomodine)*

· E ·

ELECTROLYTES

Electrolyte is actually a chemical term that refers to how a substance behaves when it is put into a solution. In horses, the word *electrolyte* is commonly applied to a variety of trace elements found in sweat, most particularly the ions of sodium, potassium, calcium and chlorine.

The loss of extensive amounts of these ions via the sweat can occur in horses, particularly during endurance-type exercise. Electrolytes in the body are responsible for the transmission of the body's electrical signals; when amounts are insufficient, weakness, disorientation and abnormal muscle function can occur.

Horses generally don't need extra electrolytes. Even in the hottest weather, horses get all the electrolytes they need in their feed.

People used to take lots of electrolytes in the form of salt pills prior to exercise. What nutritionists found was that this caused people to retain water and not sweat well, which is dangerous in hot weather. Horse feed is loaded with electrolytes and supplementation is usually not needed in ordinary circumstances.

It is, however, possible to make a horse sweat out a significant portion of his electrolytes by riding him hard in hot weather and not stopping to rest him or to give him water. During a hundred-mile endurance ride, for example, it's probably a good idea to give your horse extra electrolytes along with lots of water. Indeed, providing water, glucose and electrolytes to working endurance horses does seem to delay fatigue in these animals. Horses lose water much faster than they do electrolytes when they exercise, however, and no matter how many electrolytes you give your horse in hot weather, if you don't let him have water you're going to have some real trouble.

EMOLLIENTS

Emollients are fatty substances which are generally applied to the skin or hoof of the horse. Emollients tend to make the skin feel softer because they penetrate into the surface layers of the skin (they go no deeper). They also tend to interfere with the loss of water by the skin or surface tissues.

Emollient effects are not necessarily beneficial. The retention of water and the exclusion of air that is caused by a layer of emollient may actually be favorable to the growth of bacteria that do not require oxygen (anaerobic bacteria). Additionally, rubbing the skin while applying emollients may actually help spread bacteria and debris.

Emollient agents are commonly used to help make various over-the-counter preparations such as hoof ointments, wound treatments and liniments. Contrary to popular belief, emollients do not help medications penetrate the skin, nor do they help "draw out" toxic substances from below the skin.

Commonly used emollients in the horse include castor oil, cotton-seed oil, glycerin, lanolin and petrolatum (see various headings).

ENZYMES

Enzymes are proteins that increase the speed of the various chemical reactions that occur in the horse's body (this process is called catalysis). Enzymes are needed for many of the body's functions. The most obvious function of enzymes is in the digestive process, where enzymes help break down plant proteins so that the component amino acids can be absorbed.

Some feed supplements for the horse add digestive enzymes to the usual mix of vitamins, minerals and amino acids. Enzymes such as amylase, lipase, cellulase and pepsin are without question important for the horse's normal digestive function. However, not all digestion in the horse occurs as a result of enzymes.

The problem with the idea of adding enzymes to horse feed is that they are proteins. The horse's body breaks down proteins as a part of the digestive process. The breakdown begins in the horse's stomach, where the proteins are confronted with, among other things, hydrochloric acid. Whether or not supplemental enzymes can pass through the stomach and maintain their effectiveness is questionable.

Horse digestion is quite complex. In addition to the enzymes and stomach acids, in the upper part of the horse's digestive tract, horses also use bacteria that live in the posterior part of their digestive system to ferment feed (much like cattle do in the front part of their digestive tracts). The feed that the horse eats is therefore actually subjected to two different digestive processes. This digestive process is rather efficient and allows horses to get nutrients from things that people could never eat, like hay, for example.

Enzyme deficiencies have never been demonstrated in the horse. The benefits of adding additional enzymes to the horse's diet are certainly open to question.

EPSOM SALTS   *(Magnesium Sulfate)*

Epsom salts are available as a bulk salt that must be dissolved in water prior to use. Epsom salts have two primary uses in the horse. They are commonly used for soothing and treatment of local infection or inflammation, particularly in the hoof. They are also used by some veterinarians in the treatment of abdominal pain (colic), particularly in the treatment of intestinal impactions.

In the treatment of colic, epsom salts serve to draw water into the intestine by a process called osmosis. Oral dosing of epsom salts is usually accompanied by intravenous fluid administration to help increase this osmotic effect. Undiluted epsom salts can damage the intestinal lining. They must be mixed with water prior to administration by a nasogastric tube. Redosing may be needed for severe impactions.

In people, epsom salts are commonly placed in hot water and used as a therapeutic bath. They make the skin feel smoother and softer and are also promoted to help soothe tired or sore muscles (this may also be an effect of the hot water). In horses, probably as a result of man's experience with himself, epsom salt "soaks" are commonly recommended for the treatment of conditions of the lower limbs, especially conditions of the horse's foot, such as bruising and abscesses.

What benefit comes from soaking a horse's foot in epsom salts and water is hard to say. There would certainly be no osmotic effect exerted on abscesses through the hoof that would "draw" abscesses to the surface, since the hoof has no circulation and is not freely permeable to water. In the treatment of foot abscesses, some benefit may be obtained by the indirect cleaning of the abscess by the epsom salt solution; solutions of other substances, such as povidone-iodine, should work equally well in this regard. It is hard to conceive of any negative effect of epsom salt treatment of the horse's foot, however.

PRECAUTIONS   Therapy for intestinal impactions probably should not go on for more than three days because epsom salts can inflame the intestines. It is also theoretically possible to cause magnesium intoxication with repeated doses of epsom salts.

Some horses will not allow their hooves to be soaked in epsom salt solutions. It may not be worth the trouble.

EQUIMATE   *(Fluprostenol; see Prostaglandins and the Reproductive Cycle of the Mare)*

EQUIPOISE *(see Boldenone Undecylenate)*

EQVALAN *(see Ivermectin)*

ERYTHROMYCIN

Erythromycin is an antibiotic that is rarely used in the horse. It is most commonly supplied in the pill form for oral administration.

Erythromycin is most commonly recommended for the treatment of bacterial infections caused by *Rhodococcus equi*. This bacteria causes a particularly nasty pneumonia in foals, characterized by the formation of abscesses in the lungs. For the treatment of *Rhodococcus* infections, erythromycin is commonly used in conjuction with rifampin (see Rifampin).

SIDE EFFECTS   Erythromycin can cause severe diarrhea in horses. This may be due to some effect on the movement of the intestines. At low doses, some surgeons use erythromycin in an effort to stimulate movement of the intestines after abdominal surgery.

EUCALYPTUS OIL

Eucalyptus oil is the fragrant oil that is obtained by distilling the leaf of the eucalyptus tree with steam. It is commonly added to a variety of equine products and used in wound preparations, cough remedies, liniments and poultices.

Eucalyptus oil has mild properties as an expectorant and also inhibits the growth of bacteria. Because it smells good, it is also used as a flavoring agent.

EXPECTORANT

Expectorant agents are used to help remove secretions or exudate from the respiratory tract of the horse. They are commonly used in the treatment of cough. Expectorants attempt to reduce the thickness of secretions from the lungs and help make easier their removal by normal action of the respiratory tract. Alternatively, they may help increase the production of normal mucus.

Expectorant effects can be caused in a variety of pharmacological ways, including sedative, stimulant (irritant) and acting on the central nervous system. In horses, the majority of the products used for their expectorant action are either stimulant (irritant) or sedative in effect. Expectorants that act on the central nervous system of the horse, such as codeine, are not used.

A number of substances have stimulant (irritant) expectorant actions. Those commonly used in the horse include ammonium chloride, guaifenesin (glyceryl guaiacolate), sodium iodide, pine oil, potassium iodide and eucalyptus oil (see various headings).

Sedative expectorants that are used in the horse include potassium iodide (it has two effects), acetylcysteine and saline expectorants. The latter two agents are commonly used in inhalant or vaporizer therapy.

· F ·

FAT

Fat is commonly added to horse diets as an energy supplement. A measure of fat has almost two-and-a-half times as much energy as does the same amount of carbohydrate. Fat is readily consumed by horses and it is an excellent source of additional energy for things such as growth, weight gain and exercise. Fat adds energy to the diet without adding extra bulk. This is an advantage for horses that burn large amounts of calories, such as endurance horses. As much as twenty percent of the horse's dietary calories have been fed as fat with no apparent ill effects.

Fat is most commonly added to horse diets in the form of oils, especially corn oil. Soybean oil has also been used in experimental studies. Rice bran is also fed as a fat supplement; it only contains approximately twenty percent fat, much less than the oils, but horses seem to like the stuff.

FATTY ACIDS

Fatty acids are the raw dietary materials for many of the hormones in the horse's body, including prostaglandins (see Prostaglandin). Several of them are considered "essential" because the horse's body can't manufacture them. Essential fatty acids have to be supplied from dietary sources.

Fatty acids are the components of fat. Fat is a dietary essential and a nutritional supplement for the horse (see Fat). The exact requirements for fatty acids in the horse have not been established, but all horse feeds appear to obtain adequate quantities of fatty acids for normal functioning of the horse's system.

Insufficient amounts of fatty acids have been associated with poor hair coat quality and poor skin health in other species but not in the horse. Regular grooming is a sure way to help improve the horse's appearance.

FEBANTEL   *Rintal*

Febantel is an antiparasitic agent for the control of intestinal parasites in the horse. It is available as a paste for oral dosing or as a liquid for administration via nasogastric intubation (stomach tube). Febantel is converted to two benzimidazole-type antiparasitic agents by the body and kills parasites in the same manner as this class of drugs, by inter-fering with their energy-generating mechanisms (see Benzimidazole).

Febantel kills most intestinal parasites of the horse with the excep-tion of bots and tapeworms. It does not kill larval forms of parasites.

Febantel has been tested on pregnant mares and on stallions and no adverse effects on these animals have been shown. It may be used at any time during gestation.

PRECAUTIONS   Single overdoses of up to forty times the recom-mended dose have not been associated with any adverse effects in the horse.

FERROUS SULFATE

Ferrous sulfate is an iron-containing compound. In man, it is com-monly used in the treatment of iron deficiency anemias. Externally, it is used as a mild disinfectant.

Ferrous sulfate is a component of an over-the-counter coolant gel sold for use on the limbs of horses. What beneficial effect it might have is unknown.

FISH OIL

Fish oil is an oil produced from a variety of fish species. It is similar in effects to cod liver oil (see Cod Liver Oil).

FLUNIXIN MEGLUMINE   *Banamine*

Flunixin is another of the nonsteroidal anti-inflammatory agents used in the horse. It comes as a sterile solution for intramuscular or intrave-nous injection, or in a paste or powder for oral administration. It is recommended for the relief of pain and inflammation associated with disorders of the musculoskeletal system in the horse. It is also commonly used for the treatment of pain associated with the gastrointestinal system (colic).

According to one study, flunixin appears to be approximately four times more potent in its effects than phenylbutazone on a milligram-per-milligram basis. This potency is not any particular advantage, however. The recommended milligram dose of the drug is one-fourth that of phenylbutazone.

The anti-inflammatory effects of flunixin last for twelve to twenty-four hours after a single injection—long after the drug ceases to be detectable in the system by a blood test. The drug can be detected by urine analysis for up to forty-eight hours after administration, however.

While flunixin is useful for the treatment of colic pain, its effects are certainly less pronounced than are those of xylazine or detomodine (see entries for those drugs). For relief of severe colic pain, those are certainly the drugs of choice. Flunixin does appear to be a better choice for the treatment of colic pain than are other drugs of the same class, however. Some veterinarians report that flunixin "masks" colic pain and makes the decision for surgical intervention more difficult; experimental evidence makes this opinion difficult to understand. Nevertheless, horses referred for surgery should have a record of the treatment given to them prior to referral provided to the surgeon in attendance.

Flunixin is also useful in the treatment of endotoxic shock, a condition occasionally seen and associated with severe gastrointestinal infection and inflammation. It is also one of the most potent anti-inflammatory drugs for the relief of inflammation of the eye.

Finally, in reproductive medicine, flunixin is commonly given in management of twin pregnancies, when one twin is "pinched" by rectal palpation in hopes that the other will remain viable. The flunixin is given in an effort to reduce inflammation in the uterus after the "pinch" and to hopefully prevent abortion of the remaining fetus. The effect of flunixin on pregnant mares or fetuses has not been determined, however, management of twins in this fashion has not been associated with any adverse effects on the mare or foal.

PRECAUTIONS   Horses with known liver or kidney damage should be monitored closely if on flunixin. It should be used carefully in conjunction with aminoglycoside antibiotics (e.g., gentamycin sulfate or amikacin sulfate) because it increases the potential for these drugs to have toxic effects on the kidneys. Caution should be used in giving flunixin to weak, anemic, dehydrated or debilitated animals. Animals under thirty days of age have difficulty in metabolizing and eliminating flunixin.

There are regulations regarding the use of flunixin for horses involved in shows and competitions.

SIDE EFFECTS   When used for the conditions intended and in the manner directed, few clinical complications are reported with flunixin. About six times the IV dose in ponies, for five consecutive days, produces signs of toxicosis. As with all drugs of this class, overdose can produce signs of gastrointestinal ulceration. When flunixin is used intramuscularly, there are isolated reports of muscle swelling, soreness and abscessation. Allergic reactions to the drug have also been infrequently reported.

FLUPROSTENOL   *(see Prostaglandins and the Reproductive Cycle of the Mare)*

FOLIC ACID

Folic acid is one of the group of B-vitamins. It is important for normal red blood cell function in the horse. Folic acid is synthesized by the bacteria living in the horse's intestines in ample quantities to prevent deficiencies, even when a diet is fed that has been made deficient in folic acid. Bacterial production of folic acid in the intestines also prevents deficiencies when drugs that inhibit folic acid synthesis, such as the sulfa antibacterial drugs, are used to treat infections. Signs of toxicities or deficiencies of folic acid have not been reported in the horse.

Studies have been done regarding the effects of folic acid on the horse's hemoglobin (the protein in red blood cells that carries oxygen). In one study, exercising horses were found to have lower levels of folic acid than pregnant mares or pastured ponies; stabled horses tended to have lower folic acid levels than did horses in pasture in another study. One horse that had performed poorly at the racetrack reportedly responded positively to supplementation with folic acid. After injection of folic acid, increases in serum folic acid and red blood cell levels were observed in one study, but this effect disappeared in twenty-four hours.

Folic acid supplements appear to be poorly absorbed by the horse. Injectable solutions of folic acid are not generally available for use in the horse.

FULVACIN   *(see Griseofulvin)*

FURACIN, FURA-SEPTIN, FURAZONE   *(see Nitrofurazone)*

FUROSEMIDE   *Lasix*

Furosemide is undoubtedly the most commonly used diuretic agent in horses. It comes as a sterile solution for intravenous injection.

Although furosemide has other therapeutic applications, it is most commonly used in an attempt to prevent exercise-induced pulmonary hemorrhage (EIPH; "bleeder"). This is a condition that is most commonly seen in racehorses, although it has been seen in performance horses of other occupations. Studies have shown that furosemide is only marginally effective at reducing the incidence of exercise-induced pulmonary hemorrhage in horses.

Furosemide is a controversial drug in some circles. In addition to its diuretic effects, some studies have suggested that it may improve racing performance. Effects of furosemide have been noted in the cardiovascular, respiratory and renal systems in the horse.

PRECAUTIONS   The AHSA considers furosemide a drug that "masks" the presence of other drugs in the horse's system. Its use is prohibited in horses competing under the rules of the association. Furosemide use is also prohibited by racing associations in some states.

Specific toxicity studies on furosemide have not been performed on horses.

SIDE EFFECTS   Excessive use of furosemide can lead to fluid and electrolyte imbalances, particularly potassium deficiencies.

· G ·

GENTAMYCIN SULFATE   *Gentocin*

Gentamycin is one of a group of antibiotics known as aminoglycosides (see Amikacin). Gentamycin comes as a sterile solution that can be administered by IM or IV injection. It is also commonly infused into the uterus of mares to treat intrauterine infections and is technically only approved for use in this manner. It has been used to treat urinary, respiratory and reproductive tract infections and also for infections of the skin and soft tissues. Gentamycin solutions and ointments are available for treatment of conditions of the horse's eye. Finally, numerous combinations of gentamycin and corticosteroid products are available to treat infections accompanied by inflammation of the eye, ear and skin (see Corticosteroid).

PRECAUTIONS   Gentamycin is generally safe and effective when used as directed. The drug can be used in show horses that are at competitions. It should not be used in pregnant mares, due to the potential for kidney impairment and toxicity to the nerves of hearing of the fetus. Because only certain bacteria are killed by gentamycin, it is generally recommended that an attempt be made to isolate the bacteria causing the infection to assure that gentamycin therapy is appropriate.

SIDE EFFECTS   Aminoglycoside antibiotics (like gentamycin) have two primary side effects. First, they can damage the centers of hearing and balance. Second, they may impair function of the kidneys. Horses that have suspect kidney function, such as those that are dehydrated, or very young with immature kidneys, should be monitored closely if this drug is chosen to treat an infection. Care should be taken when gentamycin is used with nonsteroidal anti-inflammatory drugs because of the increased potential for kidney-related side effects.

GENTIAN VIOLET   *(see Crystal Violet)*

GLYCERIN

Glycerin is a clear, thick, colorless liquid with the consistency of syrup. Glycerin is actually just a type of alcohol (see Alcohol). It first came into use in medicine in about 1846.

The valuable uses of glycerin in the pharmaceutical industry are mostly as a solvent and a preservative for drugs. Glycerin is also a moistening agent (humectant). It tends to attract water; as such, it is a frequently used emollient for the skin. It has a pleasant taste as well. Many liniment, cough and poultice preparations made for the horse contain glycerin for these reasons.

Glycerin is frequently applied to the legs of the horse in so-called sweat wraps (see Sweat Wrap).

GREEN SOAP

Green soap is a cleansing soap that contains potassium. It is made from a variety of vegetable oils. The green color can come from the oils from which it is made (such as green olive oil). Curiously, the "official" green soap is not green in color. It is very mild and nonirritating.

Green soap is a detergent that is used to cleanse the skin of greasy substances. It has limited, if any, antiseptic effect. Green soap is a component of a popular liniment bath for horses.

GRISEOFULVIN   *Fulvacin*

Griseofulvin is given to the horse for the treatment and control of fungal skin infections. It comes in packets of powder for oral administration.

Griseofulvin is incorporated into the skin layers as the skin cells grow and replace themselves. Thus, the skin becomes toxic to any fungus that is living on it.

Unfortunately, the correct dosage of griseofulvin for horses has never been adequately determined and its effectiveness is unknown. Experience in other species would suggest that for griseofulvin to be effective it should be given for thirty to sixty days. Some practitioners give large weekly doses; most authorities feel that this is inappropriate.

GUAIACOL

Guaiacol is obtained from creosote. It has some use as an expectorant and a local anesthetic in man.

In horses, guaiacol is a component of a popular over-the-counter poultice preparation (see Poultice). Its usefulness or purpose is unknown in this type of medication.

· H ·

HEMLOCK OIL   (see Pine Oil)

HOOF DRESSINGS

An amazing variety of preparations are available to apply to horse hooves. Hoof dressings are painted or rubbed onto the hoof in an effort to improve hoof quality and hoof pliability ("suppleness"). At least one over-the-counter hoof dressing even purports to increase hoof growth.

Hoof tissue is largely comprised of a hard, dead protein known as keratin. Since hoof tissue is dead, it has no metabolic function and no ability to maintain itself. Hoof has a very important function, of course, in protecting the bones and sensitive structures of the horse's foot.

Ideally, horse hoof is firm, pliable and not brittle. Unfortunately, many horses are not lucky enough to have "ideal" hooves. Since the horse's hoof is so important, if it is perceived as less than ideal in quality, horse owners commonly try to improve it by using hoof dressings, hoof supplements or both.

Hoof quality is dramatically affected by the horse's environment. Either dry or moist conditions can affect it. Dry conditions tend to dehydrate hoof tissue. Moist conditions can cause hoof to soften or lose surface cells, much like when your hand stays in water for too long and the skin becomes waterlogged.

Hoof dressings are largely composed of the following ingredients: lanolin, various oils, water, stearic acid derivatives, cetyl alcohol, methyl- and propylparaben and petrolatum. These agents all act as emollients or as ointment bases (see Emollients). Presumably, just about any oily or emollient substance would have the same effect on horse hoof: helping to maintain water content. No clinical studies have been performed on hoof dressing products to see what effect they might have. They certainly are popular, though.

The addition of substances such as vitamins and protein to various hoof dressings would seem to be of little use. Since hoof tissue is dead anyway, no amount of vitamins or proteins will serve to bring it back to life. Certainly, applying anything to the dead surface tissue of the hoof will not help speed or improve hoof growth.

Mild "blisters" of the coronary band are occasionally recommended to increase the speed of hoof growth (see Blister). Evidently, by inflaming the coronary band, it is hoped that hoof growth will be accelerated, presumably by increasing circulation to the coronary band. There is no evidence that this treatment is effective.

HOOF SUPPLEMENTS

In addition to things that are put on the hoof (see Hoof Dressings, above), things are also put in the horse (in the feed) in attempts to improve hoof growth and quality. Substances commonly added to the horse's diet to "help" hoof growth include: biotin, methionine, gelatin and various vitamins and minerals (see various headings). Experimentally, biotin has been the only feed additive that has shown some effectiveness in improving hoof quality.

HUMAN CHORIONIC GONADOTROPIN   *(hCG)*

Human chorionic gonadotropin is a hormone that is used in reproductive management of the broodmare. It comes as a sterile powder
that is mixed with sterile water to provide a solution for IM or IV
administration.

When it is injected into mares, hCG has been demonstrated to
reduce the length of the heat cycle by two to four days. Within forty-
eight hours after injection of hCG in susceptible mares, the ovaries are
stimulated to release an egg (ovulation). Human chorionic gonadotropin works best when the follicle on the ovary (the follicle is the
structure from which the egg is produced) is of an appropriate size,
usually no sooner than day two or three after the beginning of estrus
(heat). This effect on ovulation is very useful when trying to decrease
the number of inseminations per heat cycle or when trying to time
mating and the release of the egg by the mare's ovary.

PRECAUTIONS   Human chorionic gonadotropin is a protein obtained from the urine of pregnant women. Because it is a protein, it
has the potential to stimulate an immune response to it by the horse's
body. While this is not harmful to the horse, it can cause the drug to
be ineffective, since the antibodies produced by the horse to hCG can
neutralize the effect of the drug. Therefore, it has been suggested that
no more than two injections of hCG should be given to any one mare
during the same breeding season.

SIDE EFFECTS   No significant adverse effects in horses after the
use of hCG have been reported.

HYALURONIC ACID   *(Sodium Hyaluronate) Synacid, Hylartin-V, Equron, Hyalovet, Legend*

Hyaluronic acid is used in the treatment and control of joint inflammation in the horse. It is available as a sterile solution for injection

into the joint (intra-articular or IA injection). A preparation of hyaluronic acid is also available for intravenous administration. For the treatment of tendon and ligament injuries, injection both into and beside these structures has been discussed.

Most synthetic hyaluronic acid is derived from purified rooster combs. It is a naturally occurring substance in the horse's body, and is found in particularly high concentrations in joints, tendon sheaths and the eye.

In joints, naturally occurring hyaluronic acid functions as a "boundary" lubricant. A joint occurs anywhere that bone meets bone. Around the joint is nonbone ("soft") tissue that includes the membrane of the joint (the synovial membrane). Hyaluronic acid is thought to act as a lubricant at the boundary between the soft tissue of the joint and the joint cartilage (the covering of the ends of the bones in a joint) as the joint bends and moves.

Synthetic forms of hyaluronic acid have a number of beneficial effects that have been demonstrated after injection into the joint. Most obviously, joint lubrication is improved after IA injection of hyaluronic acid.

Hyaluronic acid is a large molecule. Because of its size, it can apparently impede the movement into the joint of inflammatory compounds by sort of crowding them out (this phenomenon is known as steric hindrance). Additionally, hyaluronic acid has a direct anti-inflammatory effect caused by picking up and removing by-products of inflammation (like DMSO does) and by an anti-prostaglandin effect (like the nonsteroidal anti-inflammatory drugs). These anti-inflammatory effects may also be advantageous in the treatment of tendon and ligament injuries. Finally, in the laboratory, hyaluronic acid has been demonstrated to stimulate the production of more normal joint fluid by inflamed cells from the joint membrane.

There are differences among the various hyaluronic acid products used in joints (of which there are many), the chief ones being cost and molecular weight. The two differences seem to be directly related to each other, that is, the higher the molecular weight of the product, the more it costs. High-molecular-weight hyaluronic acid is purported to hinder the entrance of inflammatory molecules into joints more effectively than do lower-weight compounds. Additionally, after joint surgery, higher-weight compounds may have more value than lower-weight compounds because they may tend to inhibit the production of fibrous tissue in the joint. Clinically, however, the two compounds seem to be equally effective in the treatment of inflamed joints.

Injected into the joint, hyaluronic acid is quite safe and no adverse effects are seen at five times overdose.

The intravenous preparation of hyaluronic acid was approved for use in the horse in 1993. Unlike the preparations for use in the joint, the hyaluronic acid in this preparation comes from a microbial source rather than rooster combs (although this fact is probably not that important). In the clinical study done to test the drug, forty-six horses with lameness of the fetlock or knee joints (metacarpophalangeal and carpal joints, respectively) were treated with intravenous hyaluronic acid. One, two or three injections were given. Improvement was reported in ninety percent of the cases. Some surgeons prefer to use this form of the drug immediately post-surgery, rather than direct injection into the joint. How, why or if intravenous hyaluronic acid is consistently effective for treatment of joint inflammation in the horse is not apparent at this time, although its use is being investigated.

PRECAUTIONS   After injection of hyaluronic acid, either in the joint or in the vein, resting the horse is generally recommended prior to gradually resuming normal athletic activity.

SIDE EFFECTS Injection of hyaluronic acid into a joint may cause acute inflammation of the joint (known as joint flare). Signs of joint flare include heat, swelling and pain of the affected joint. This effect is usually temporary but it must be distinguished from joint infections, a serious result that is possible following injection of any substance into a joint.

Injection of any foreign substance into a joint should be preceded by proper procedures to ensure cleanliness and help prevent infection, such as clipping of the hair, disinfectant scrubbing of the joint surfaces and the wearing of latex gloves by the person doing the injecting.

No adverse side effects were reported in the clinical trials of horses receiving the intravenous preparation of hyaluronic acid.

HYDROGEN PEROXIDE

Hydrogen peroxide is a germicide that people use a lot when they see a wound in their horse. Hydrogen peroxide kills bacteria by releasing tissue oxygen. The release of oxygen is why, when hydrogen peroxide is applied to a wound, the surface of the wound bubbles and foams.

Hydrogen peroxide is actually quite weak in its antibacterial effects. However, the foaming action makes it look very dramatic. The foaming can help get debris out of areas that are not easily reached by scrubbing.

Contrary to popular usage and belief, hydrogen peroxide is generally *not* recommended for the treatment of fresh wounds, for a variety of reasons that have to do with its damaging effects on the tissue and small blood vessels. Antiseptic solutions such as chlorhexidine and povidone-iodine are probably better choices for the cleansing of fresh wounds (see Wound Treatments).

HYDROXYZINE

Hydroxyzine is an antihistamine. It is available in a tablet for oral consumption by the horse.

Hydroxyzine has shown some beneficial effects in the treatment and control of allergic reactions such as urticaria ("hives") and conditions characterized by rubbing and itching (see Antihistamine).

No significant side effects or precautions have been reported with the use of hydroxyzine. The use of the drug is prohibited in horses competing under AHSA regulations.

· I ·

ICHTHAMMOL

Ichthammol is a mild skin irritant and local antibacterial agent. It also has emollient (softening or soothing) and demulcent (soothing or alleviating irritation) properties. It is a medication that has been around for many years.

Ichthammol is made from shale, which is hydrocarbon-containing rock. The hydrocarbon base gives it the characteristic "tar-like" odor. The "ichth" in ichthammol is from the Greek word for fish; the first shales used in the production of ichthammol had fossilized impressions of fish in them, hence the name.

Ichthammol is supplied as an ointment for external application to the skin only. Ichthammol may also be applied under a bandage. Ichthammol is commonly used as a poultice-type agent (see Poultice), under the assumption that it promotes the absorption of swellings by the horse's body. There is no evidence that it actually has this sort of effect.

Ichthammol tends to toughen the sole of the hoof when applied to it.

IODINE

Iodine is one of the basic elements in nature. It is essential for proper functioning of the thyroid gland. Very small amounts are required for normal thyroid function. Normal horse diets supply ample amounts of dietary iodine.

In horses, liquid tincture of iodine is used because of its germicidal properties. It comes as a seven percent solution for application to wounds. Iodine solutions can be quite caustic and irritating, however, and should be applied to wounds only after careful consideration. In addition, because iodine stains so badly, it is not a popular treatment of wounds of the horse.

Iodine is a component of various liniment and hoof preparations, where its particular effects are unknown. Iodine also reportedly tends to help dry the hoof and many horse owners use it to toughen a horse's sole. When it is applied to the horse's foot, care must be taken to avoid getting excessive amounts on and around the coronary band. Iodine can irritate and inflame this area.

Iodine is also a component of some over-the-counter medications sold for the treatment of thrush.

IODOFORM

Iodoform is an iodine preparation. It was once widely used as a skin ointment to take advantage of the germicidal properties of iodine (see Iodine).

Iodoform is a component of an over-the-counter preparation used for the treatment of wounds of the horse. It is less caustic than iodine and tends to stain less. It is not widely used by veterinarians.

IRON

Iron is an essential element for oxygen transport by the horse's body. The highest levels of iron are found in the body's red blood cells.

Iron supplements are commonly given to horses to act as "blood builders," that is, in an effort to increase the production of red blood cells by the horse's body. This is another case where if some is good, more is not necessarily better. It is virtually impossible to create a diet in horses that is deficient in iron. Additional dietary iron does not stimulate the production of red blood cells nor of hemoglobin, the protein in red blood cells that carries oxygen.

Iron-containing tonics and supplements are frequently given to horses that have been diagnosed with anemia (a decrease in the number of red blood cells). True anemias occur very rarely in the horse. Horses have a large number of red blood cells in the spleen. Routine blood tests do not measure these cells. Horses are able to double the number of their red blood cells, almost literally at a moment's notice, due to this reserve of splenic blood cells. Accordingly, routine blood tests that seem to indicate a slight reduction in the number of red blood cells probably do not reflect a true anemia, especially in a horse that seems otherwise healthy (eating, performing, etc). A depression in red blood cell levels can be associated with some chronic disease states, but it is usually an insignificant variation from normal levels. True anemias in the horse must be treated aggressively and do not respond to iron supplementation.

Iron supplementation is of little value in the horse. Neither iron deficiencies nor toxicities seem to be a problem.

ISOPROPYL ALCOHOL   *(Rubbing Alcohol)*

Isopropyl alcohol is a commonly used antiseptic for the skin (see Antiseptic). It is used in a number of liniment preparations for the horse and it can be applied directly to the skin. It has no particular therapeutic benefit when "rubbed" on the skin and its effects and uses are the same as those for other alcohols (see Liniment, Alcohol).

ISOXSUPRINE HYDROCHLORIDE

Isoxsuprine is a drug that induces dilation of the peripheral blood vessels in man. Peripheral vessels are the small blood vessels that exist in extremities or in the brain; these vessels typically carry blood under very little pressure. In people, isoxsuprine is used to try to help dilate blood vessels to help relieve the effects of blood insufficiency in the brain and other tissues.

In the horse, isoxsuprine is very popular for the treatment of navicular disease. Some veterinarians feel that navicular disease is a result of problems with the circulation to the navicular bone, although the true cause of navicular disease is not well understood. In two studies, horses with navicular disease did benefit after isoxsuprine was prescribed. In another study, however, investigators were unable to show that the drug reached detectable levels in the circulation of the horse.

Importantly, the effects of isoxsuprine do not seem to depend on the dose. If the recommended dose does not work, exceeding the dose, while safe, is of no benefit.

Isoxsuprine is also prescribed by some veterinarians for the treatment of laminitis in the horse. In laminitis, abnormalities with the circulation to the feet of the horse are responsible for the development of the condition. It is reasonable to hope that a vasodilating agent would be useful in helping to treat this condition by allowing normal circulation to the foot to be maintained. No studies have been performed to evaluate the effectiveness of isoxsuprine for the treatment of laminitis, however.

PRECAUTIONS   Isoxsuprine should not be used immediately after foaling in the mare nor should it be given during bleeding episodes. This is because one would presumably not want to dilate blood vessels where the danger of bleeding already exists. The use of isoxsuprine is prohibited in horses showing under AHSA rules.

SIDE EFFECTS   Isoxsuprine is largely free of reported side effects, although hypersensitivity to the drug has been seen by the author in one horse. Interestingly, the drug is only considered as "possibly effective" by the U.S. Food and Drug Administration for the treatment of the conditions it is prescribed for in human medicine.

IVERMECTIN   *Eqvalan, Zimectrin*

Ivermectin is an antiparasitic agent available for use in the horse. It is available in a paste for oral administration or as a liquid for administration by nasogastric intubation (stomach tube). In the early 1980s a product was available for injection into the muscle, but it was withdrawn from the market.

Ivermectins work by paralyzing and killing the parasites. The worms are then expelled by the movement of the intestines. Ivermectin is extremely safe and has been tested at a ten times overdose. It has also been tested in pregnant and breeding animals and found to be safe.

One of the advantages of ivermectin is that it kills the vast majority of equine parasites, including those of the skin and bots in the stomach. It has no effect, however, against tapeworms in the horse. In addition to adult parasites, regular recommended doses of ivermectin also kill migrating parasite larvae in the bloodstream.

SIDE EFFECTS   *Onchocerca* species are parasites that live in the skin of the horse, especially around the neck, the base of the ears and the ventral midline. After treatment with ivermectin, allergic reactions, manifested by swelling and intense itching, have been seen. This is presumably due to the fact that a large number of skin parasites have been killed. While not a serious problem, horses can quickly rub out mane and tail hair from the itching. This is, of course, not desirable for show horses (see Dewormers). Ivermectin is the treatment of choice for skin conditions resulting from *Onchocerca* infestations, however.

· J ·

JUNIPER OIL   *(Juniper Tar)*

Juniper oil is a volatile oil obtained from the juniper tree. It is a mild irritant (see Counterirritant) and also has anti-itch properties that are used in man to treat such conditions as psoriasis and eczema. Juniper oil is a component of an over-the-counter liniment sold for use in the horse (see Liniment).

· K ·

KAOLIN

Kaolin is actually porcelain clay, made of aluminum silicate. It has been used as a medicinal agent since the time of the ancient Greeks. The name kaolin comes from the Chinese word for "high ridge," referring to where the clay was found.

Kaolin is used mostly for its abilities as an adsorbent (it attracts and retains materials on its surface). It is most commonly employed in the treatment of diarrhea of foals, frequently in combination with pectin, a fruit extract that is also used to thicken jellies.

Kaolin is a common component of over-the-counter poultice preparations for use on the horse's hooves and legs, presumably in hopes that its adsorbent qualities will be of some use (see Poultice).

KAOPECTATE   *(see Kaolin)*

KETAMINE HYDROCHLORIDE   *Ketaset, Vetalar*

Ketamine is a short-acting intravenous anesthetic that is used for short-term procedures requiring general anesthesia in the horse. It was first introduced in 1965 for use in man. The drug is only approved for animal use in cats and nonhuman primates but it is commonly used in horses. In man, ketamine is so safe that it is commonly used for anesthesia of children.

Prior to the use of ketamine, horses are generally given a tranquilizer to promote muscle relaxation. Xylazine is the most commonly used tranquilizing agent given prior to injection of ketamine, but anesthetic combinations of ketamine with detomodine, acepromazine and diazepam have also been reported (see those specific drugs for more information). Ketamine is also used as an inducing agent to anesthetize horses for general surgery prior to maintaining them on an anesthetic gas.

Horses that have been given ketamine do not appear to be relaxed and "asleep." Although Ketamine does not produce a deep anesthestic "sleep" the animals are adequately anesthetized and do not feel the surgical procedures (such as when stallions are castrated).

PRECAUTIONS   Ketamine should not be used to maintain anesthesia in prolonged surgical procedures. Anesthesia usually lasts about twenty minutes, at best. It should also not be used in animals with liver or kidney problems or in animals with head trauma (it elevates the pressure of the fluid around the brain). As with any anesthetic, recovery should be monitored so that horses recovering do not hurt themselves while struggling to get up.

SIDE EFFECTS   Adverse effects of ketamine are not reported in the horse. Observations such as muscle tremors, eye movements, sweating and jerking are normal in the anesthetized horse following injection of ketamine.

KETOPROFEN   *Ketofen*

Ketoprofen is another of the nonsteroidal anti-inflammatory agents available for the horse. The drug comes as a sterile solution for intravenous administration. Intramuscular administration has been reported with no adverse effects; however, intramuscular use is against the manufacturer's recommendations.

Ketoprofen is recommended for the relief of pain and inflammation associated with diseases of the musculoskeletal system. The effects of the drug appear to be maximal at about twelve hours and last for up to twenty-four hours. A 1995 study suggests that ketoprofen is more effective than phenylbutazone at relieving some types of musculoskeletal pain.

PRECAUTIONS   Ketoprofen appears to be very safe in the horse unless extreme overdoses are given. Precautions similar to those of other nonsteroidal agents would be appropriate (see Aspirin; Nonsteroidal Anti-Inflammatory Drug). The effects of ketoprofen on fertility, pregnancy and fetal health have not been studied.

Drug levels of ketoprofen have been monitored by the AHSA and found to be quite high. So far, no action has been taken in regard to specific regulations involving this drug.

SIDE EFFECTS   No significant side effects of ketoprofen have been reported during the studies done on this drug.

· L ·

LACTOBACILLUS *(see Bacterial Supplements)*

LANOLIN

Lanolin is a purified fatlike substance that comes from sheep wool. Its use was begun by Galen, the famous first-century Roman physician.

Lanolin is used primarily as a base for ointments in the horse that are applied to the skin and the hoof. Lanolin is useful as an emollient (see Emollients).

LASIX *(see Furosemide)*

LIDOCAINE HYDROCHLORIDE

Lidocaine is a local anesthetic agent for use in the horse. It is most commonly used to infiltrate wounds locally to make them numb when it is necessary to repair them with sutures. Lidocaine is used for local anesthetic "nerve blocks," used during lameness examinations and other procedures. It is also employed for anesthesia of the surface of the eye or within a joint, if anesthesia of these areas is desired. Lidocaine is used to help treat arrhythmias of the heart in most mammals, although it is rarely used for that in horses since heart disease and pathologic abnormal rhythms are uncommon in them.

Many local anesthetic agents have been developed. Lidocaine is the one that is most commonly used in the horse because it is safe and relatively inexpensive. It comes as a sterile solution for injection in the muscle, under the skin or in the vein.

Lidocaine is also combined with epinephrine in some solutions. Epinephrine, an important hormone in the horse's body, causes blood vessels to constrict when it is injected locally. Some veterinarians elect to use the combination product in an effort to control bleeding during wound repair.

PRECAUTIONS   Because lidocaine causes anesthesia of an area, it is possible that damage to anesthetized structures can occur, particularly during lameness examination. Although it happens very rarely, fractures or other injuries of horses have occurred when injured structures have been anesthetized and the horse begins to use the affected area in a normal fashion. Prior to beginning use of lidocaine (or any local anesthetic), a thorough examination of the horse should be performed to help ensure that serious conditions that could be dramatically worsened by exercise do not exist in a limb that is to be anesthetized.

Lidocaine and most other commonly used local anesthetics in the horse are chemically related to procaine. Procaine is a substance for which the AHSA tests, and horses are not permitted to have this substance in their systems during competitions. Drugs related to procaine, such as lidocaine, are detected in these tests.

SIDE EFFECTS   Lidocaine is very safe in the horse. Side effects can be seen in small animals if large amounts of the drug are absorbed, but the size of the horse usually precludes this problem.

LIME

Lime is a chemical (calcium hydroxide) that is commonly used in the manufacture of cement. It is also used as a drying agent that is spread on the bottom of wet stalls to help dry them after they are cleaned out.

Lime is the principal component of a popular over-the-counter wound preparation. As such, it is used because it has some disinfectant properties (see Disinfectant), although what possible benefit could be obtained from applying this caustic chemical to a healing wound escapes understanding.

LINIMENT *Absorbine, Vetrolin, Bigeloil*

Liniments are oily liquid preparations for use on the skin. They generally contain various combinations of alcohol, camphor, green soap, iodine, menthol and many other substances (see various headings).

As a general rule, liniments produce local skin irritation. When the skin is chemically irritated, surface blood vessels dilate. In man, this brings a feeling of warmth to the area and helps to relieve muscle and joint stiffness and soreness. Whether this same effect is produced in horses is anyone's guess.

Claims that liniments "increase circulation" to areas are not supported by any research. As a practical matter, increased circulation has not been demonstrated as a result of any therapy. Nor has any study been done to show that if circulation could be increased, it would somehow improve or speed up healing.

LINOLEIC ACID *(see Fatty Acids)*

LINSEED OIL

Linseed oil is obtained from a dried seed, as the name implies. It is a yellow, oily liquid. It is used to formulate various liniments and is also available in an over-the-counter preparation for application to wounds. Linseed oil has no recognized therapeutic properties.

LIPOIC ACID *(see Fatty Acids)*

LUTALYSE *(Dinoprost; see Prostaglandins and the Reproductive Cycle of the Mare)*

· M ·

MALATHION

Malathion is a rose and plant pesticide that is also occasionally used for the treatment of external parasites of the horse. It must be diluted prior to application to the horse's skin. It is relatively safe and nontoxic.

Horses that are intended to be shipped to Hawaii must receive a malathion bath within one week of shipment.

MECLOFENAMIC ACID   *Arquel*

Meclofenamic acid is a nonsteroidal anti-inflammatory drug that is chemically different from aspirin, phenylbutazone and the like. Its properties are similar, however, and meclofenamic acid is useful for the relief of pain and inflammation. It is an unusual drug in that it does take a while to take effect. As opposed to the several hours required for the effects of other nonsteroidal anti-inflammatory drugs to take effect, meclofenamic acid takes from thirty-six to ninety-six hours to begin working.

Meclofenamic acid is used in the treatment of acute or chronic inflammatory conditions of the musculoskeletal system in the horse. It comes as a powder for oral administration. Horses seem to eat it fairly well. The drug stays in the system long enough that once-daily administration should be adequate.

PRECAUTIONS   In one study, meclofenamic acid appeared to have no bad effects on reproductive function in the horse, nor did it have any adverse effects on developing fetuses. More information would be useful, however, before the drug could be called completely safe for use in these animals.

Signs of intolerance to meclofenamic acid include colic, diarrhea and decreased appetite. If these signs are seen in a horse being given the drug, administration should, of course, be stopped.

There are no AHSA regulations regarding the use of meclofenamic acid.

SIDE EFFECTS   At the recommended doses, adverse side effects of meclofenamic acid are rarely reported. Horses have been kept on the drug continuously for up to forty-two days and intermittently for up to six months with no bad effects.

When doses of meclofenamic acid are increased above the recommended levels, however, the number of red blood cells in the circulation is observed to reduce; blood may also appear in the feces. Horses with infestations of bots, a common parasite of the stomach of the horse, should be given meclofenamic acid with caution. Mild colic and a change in the consistency of the manure has been seen in horses that were heavily infested with bots and had been given meclofenamic acid.

MENTHOL

Menthol is an alcohol obtained from the oils of a variety of mints. It smells like peppermint.

Since the smell is pleasant and recognizable, menthol is used in many preparations sold over the counter for horses. It has some effectiveness as an anti-itching agent and as a counterirritant (see Counterirritant). Because of its volatile and pleasant smell, menthol is also used for relief of nasal congestion (it is used to make cough drops in man). It is used in a variety of liniments and cough medications for the horse (see Liniment).

MEPIVACAINE HYDROCHLORIDE *Carbocaine*

Mepivacaine is chemically related to lidocaine and is roughly equal to that drug in potency and toxicity. It comes as a sterile solution and can be used for local nerve blocks, injection in the spinal canal (epidural), injection in joints, as a topical spray and for infiltrating wounds.

A recent study has shown that the onset of joint anesthesia with mepivacaine begins approximately five minutes after injection and lasts for approximately fifty-five minutes. Mepivacaine apparently does not have a longer-lasting effect than lidocaine, as some people believe (see Lidocaine).

METHIONINE

Methionine is a sulfur-containing amino acid. Amino acids are the building blocks from which proteins are made. Methionine is found in high concentrations in horse hoof. Accordingly, a variety of hoof supplements have been devised which include methionine, apparently in the belief that if some methionine is needed for normal hoof, additional amounts will make the hoof even better.

Methionine deficiencies have not been demonstrated in the horse. Supplementation with methionine to improve hoof quality has largely been disappointing in its results (see Amino Acid).

METHOCARBAMOL *Robaxin*

Methocarbamol is used for the relief of inflammation and muscle spasm and to cause muscle relaxation in horses. It is used in the treatment of such conditions as muscle injury and rhabdomyolysis (myositis or "tying up") and for maintaining muscle relaxation in horses afflicted with tetanus. Methocarbamol is available as a sterile solution for intravenous injection in horses. An oral tablet is also commonly given to horses; however, no studies have been done on horses to determine what, if any, dose of methocarbamol given orally is effective.

PRECAUTIONS   The effects of methocarbamol on breeding animals have not been determined.

Like most muscle-relaxing agents, methocarbamol has the potential to cause sedation in the horse. Because of this effect, the drug has been used in an effort to calm horses, particularly those used for performance. The use of methocarbamol is therefore controlled according to the regulations of the AHSA.

Intravenous methocarbamol should not be given to horses with kidney failure because the vehicle in which the drug is carried in solution can be potentially harmful if kidney function is impaired.

SIDE EFFECTS   Few adverse side effects of methocarbamol are reported. Methocarbamol appears to be quite safe and nontoxic. The drug appears safe at up to eight times overdose. Salivation, weakness and stumbling are reported effects in small animals.

METHYL SALICYLATE   *(Wintergreen Oil)*

Methyl salicylate can be made synthetically or by distilling the leaves of plants that contain this compound. Methyl salicylate is a compound that is useful in the manufacture of various preparations for the horse, such as wound treatments, liniments and poultices. It is considered to have little or no therapeutic value on its own, however.

Methyl salicylate is considered a flavoring agent. It smells like wintergreen candy. It has some use as a mild counterirritant (see Counterirritant).

METHYLENE BLUE

Methylene blue is a chemical dye that is available as a treatment for superficial wounds in the horse. Other than turning them blue, it has no known effect on wounds.

METHYLPARABEN

Methylparaben is a preservative agent with antifungal properties. It is used to help preserve cosmetic preparations that contain fats and oils. It is found in a variety of hoof dressings for horses. These contain high quantities of various oils (see Hoof Dressings). In high concentrations, methylparaben also has an antiseptic effect.

METHYLPREDNISOLONE ACETATE   *Depo-Medrol*

Methylprednisolone is a corticosteroid preparation that is most commonly injected into joints for the treatment of arthritis. It comes as a sterile suspension. The drug can also be injected into inflamed areas for reduction of local swelling and inflammation.

Methylprednisolone is considered a medium- to long-acting corticosteroid. After injection into joints, drug levels have been found for up to thirty-nine days.

PRECAUTIONS   When this product is administered into a joint, the joint should be clipped of hair and surgically scrubbed with disinfectant solutions prior to injection (as with any injection into a joint).

After joint injection, horses should be rested for several days prior to a gradual return to normal use.

Occasional acute inflammation ("joint flare") is seen after injection of steroids into joints, resulting in heat, pain and swelling in the affected area. This effect usually disappears rapidly but must be distinguished from joint infections, a serious problem.

SIDE EFFECTS   Steroidal anti-inflammatory drugs such as methylprednisolone have been accused of accelerating joint destruction in horses with pre-existing arthritis. In joints, corticosteroids have been demonstrated to decrease the metabolism of cartilage cells. This can, apparently, sometimes result in accelerated deterioration of joint surfaces (steroid arthropathy). There is, however, little experimental information regarding the effects of injection of steroidal anti-inflammatory agents such as methylprednisolone into previously damaged or arthritic joints.

Considerable evidence exists that injection of corticosteroids into normal joints is not harmful to the joint surfaces, although cartilage metabolism may be affected for up to sixteen weeks after injection (see Corticosteroid).

METHYLSULFONYLMETHANE *(MSM)*

Methylsulfonylmethane is a dietary supplement for which the only proven use for the horse is as a source of the mineral sulfur . Sulfur is a trace mineral that is found in a variety of proteins in the body. Sulfur deficiencies are unknown in the horse.

Methylsulfonylmethane is a by-product of the chemical breakdown of dimethyl sulfoxide (DMSO) by the body (see DMSO). Because of this fact, many people have promoted MSM as a "dietary form" of DMSO. That is, they say that MSM will go throughout the body to help pick up and neutralize anti-inflammatory compounds (DMSO does have some potent anti-inflammatory properties). There is no scientific evidence to support claims that MSM has this effect.

METRONIDAZOLE *Flagyl*

Metronidazole is an antimicrobial drug. It is available as a pill for oral administration to the horse.

Metronidazole is primarily used to treat infections caused by bacteria that cannot live in the presence of oxygen (anaerobic bacteria). Anaerobic infections are most commonly seen in the horse's chest; the disease is called pleuropneumonia or "shipping fever." The drug is usually used along with other antibiotics but is very effective in treating anaerobic infections.

A recent report advocates the use of a paste made from metronidazole for the treatment of "canker," an infectious condition of the horse's hoof. The paste, which was specially formulated for the study, was very effective in treating this difficult condition.

There are no known precautions or side effects accompanying the use of metronidazole in the horse.

MINERAL

A mineral is an inorganic substance that is needed for normal metabolic and biologic activity. Minerals cannot, as is the case with vitamins, be formed in the body. Minerals must be present in the food or be supplemented.

Most feeds normally given to horses are rich sources of minerals. Mineral supplementation in the horse's diet is usually not needed. However, it is common practice to provide horses with a trace mineral block that also contains salt (sodium chloride). This practice is certainly harmless, although if the horse decides to pass the time by eating his mineral block, it can be expensive. Mineral supplementation can also be provided in a variety of over-the-counter preparations. The toxicity of most minerals is, fortunately, quite low (see also Chelated Minerals).

MINERAL OIL

Light mineral oil is commonly given to horses for the treatment of abdominal pain (colic). Mineral oil is commonly thought of as an intestinal lubricant, allowing masses blocking the intestine to "slip by" more easily. In fact, the effects of mineral oil are not completely understood. Mineral oil may function by blocking the absorption of water by the intestines (oil and water do not mix). It would thereby indirectly increase the amount of water in the intestines. The increased water would then tend to promote softening of hard masses. Additionally, mineral oil might serve as an irritant to the intestinal wall. In this manner, it would serve to actually promote water excretion by the intestine, which would also tend to soften the consistency of feces.

PRECAUTIONS   Mineral oil may be given in the feed. Veterinarians most commonly give it by nasogastric intubation (stomach tube). Of course, care must be used when giving mineral oil in this fashion. If the nasogastric tube is placed in the trachea instead of the esophagus and mineral oil is accidentally given into the lung, fatal pneumonias are usually the result.

It is possible for mineral oil to pass around masses in the intestines. Although the appearance of mineral oil around the anus is generally a good sign that the horse's colic is resolving, if clinical signs of colic persist, the horse should be re-examined by a veterinarian.

Mineral oil should not be used in combination with DSS (see Dioctyl Sodium Sulfosuccinate), a stool softener. Theoretically, the combination of the two substances may allow for the absorption of mineral oil into the bloodstream.

Some veterinarians do not like to use mineral oil in horses that may require surgery to correct their colic. They feel that mineral oil may interfere with surgery or make a clean surgery more difficult. However, most surgeons feel that mineral oil in the intestine does not adversely affect the surgical process or outcome.

SIDE EFFECTS   Mineral oil is very bland and very safe to use.

· N ·

NAPROXEN

Naproxen is a nonsteroidal anti-inflammatory agent for the treatment of musculoskeletal disorders in the horse. It is no longer manufactured specifically for use in the horse, but a generic pill form is available. It was previously available specifically for horses in a sterile solution for intravenous administration and in a powder for oral administration. Naproxen is from the same class of drugs as aspirin and phenylbutazone but is reportedly superior to either of these drugs in its anti-inflammatory effect.

Naproxen is most commonly used in the treatment of muscle soreness in the horse, such as that seen after intense exertion or associated with exertional rhabdomyolysis (myositis or "tying up").

The margin of safety of naproxen is good. Precautions and side effects are similar to those of aspirin or other nonsteroidal anti-inflammatory agents.

NAXCEL *(see Ceftiofur Sodium)*

NEATSFOOT OIL

Neatsfoot oil is a light yellow oil that is obtained from the feet and shinbones of cattle. It is primarily used to treat leather.

Neatsfoot oil is also found as a component of various hoof dressings in the horse (see Hoof Dressings). The oil presumably has some emollient qualities (see Emollients).

NEOMYCIN *Panalog, Neo-Predef, Triple Antibiotic Ointment, Neosporin, Tresaderm*

Neomycin is another of the aminoglycoside group of antibiotics that include gentamycin and amikacin (see the various headings). In horses, neomycin is most commonly found in a variety of preparations used on the skin, in the ear or in the eye. Many products contain neomycin in combination with other antibiotics, antifungal agents or corticosteroid anti-inflammatory drugs (see Corticosteroid, Bacitracin).

NIACIN (see Vitamin B-3)

NITROFURAZONE   Furacin, Fura-Septin, Fura-Zone, Nitrofur, NFZ

Nitrofurazone is one of the most commonly used antibacterial preparations for the treatment of wounds of the horse. It is available in an ointment, a liquid or a powder. Its intended use is for the treatment and control of infections of superficial wounds and abrasions. A related compound, furazolidone, is available in spray that is applied to wounds just like spray paint (e.g., Furox spray).

Nitrofurazone-based ointments are commonly used in "sweat wraps." This type of bandage is applied to affected legs in an effort to reduce swelling. The nitrofurazone ointment can be used alone, or is commonly mixed with corticosteroids and/or dimethyl sulfoxide, theoretically to increase the anti-inflammatory effect. After the ointment is applied, the limb is wrapped in plastic wrap, covered with a bandage and left for at least twenty-four hours. The observed effects of the sweat wrap may only be due to the fact that the ointment occludes the skin.

PRECAUTIONS   No ointment, spray or liquid, when applied to a wound, should be expected to completely prevent the growth of bacteria. In fact, the necessity for controlling surface infections in superficial wounds or wounds that are granulating is debatable. However, the presence of blood, plasma or pus on a wound decreases the ability of nitrofurazone to kill bacteria. Some experimental evidence suggests that nitrofurazone delays the rate of wound healing by twenty-four percent.

These drugs cannot be used systemically; that is, they cannot be given orally or by injection due to a wide variety of side effects.

SIDE EFFECTS   Although these drugs are widely used and sold over the counter, there is some concern as to their ability to cause cancer in laboratory animals. From the fact that there has been long-term and widespread use of the drug with few reported problems, there certainly would appear to be little reason for deep concern over the use of this drug. However, its cancer-causing potential is being investigated.

NONSTEROIDAL ANTI-INFLAMMATORY DRUG

Since the early 1970s, when it was discovered how aspirin works, literally hundreds of structurally different compounds collectively referred to as nonsteroidal anti-inflammatory drugs have been synthesized. These drugs are generally anti-inflammatory and analgesic (pain relieving); they also can be used to control fever.

Most nonsteroidal anti-inflammatory drugs commonly used in the horse act in a similar fashion; they block the conversion of a naturally occurring substance called arachidonic acid to another group of chemicals called prostaglandins. Among their many effects, prostaglandins are important mediators of pain and inflammation in the horse's body (see Prostaglandin).

These drugs are among the most frequently prescribed in the horse. Specific compounds that are or have been given to the horse include aspirin, phenylbutazone, meclofenamic acid, flunixin meglumine, ketoprofen and naproxen (see individual listings for these drugs).

The side effects of nonsteroidal anti-inflammatory drugs are also most likely related to their effect on prostaglandins, which are among the most widely occurring chemical compounds in the body. Although rare, side effects are most commonly seen in the gastrointestinal and renal (kidney) systems of the horse. They also occur more commonly in ponies and foals than in adult large-breed horses.

Importantly, the adverse effects of these drugs are cumulative; that is, using various members of this class of drugs together will increase the potential for adverse effects. Combination therapies of these drugs should be avoided in horses.

· O ·

OCTOCOSANOL

Octocosanol is an alcohol that is found in some vegetable oils and waxes, most notably in wheat germ oil (see Wheat Germ Oil). It has been promoted as ergogenic (improving performance and enhancing work output) in the horse. It is supposed to increase oxygen transport by the body. How it might do so is unclear.

The consensus of results on studies of octocosanol on humans is that it does not improve endurance. Its purported benefits have certainly never been demonstrated in the horse.

OLEIC ACID   *(see Fatty Acids)*

ORGOTEIN   *Palosein*

Orgotein is a nonsteroidal anti-inflammatory agent used in the treatment of soft-tissue inflammation of horses. It does not have direct pain-relieving properties. It is not related to the class of drugs that includes the majority of the pain-relieving anti-inflammatory agents used in the horse, such as phenylbutazone.

Orgotein is one of a group of drugs known as dismutases. These drugs are thought to remove free oxygen radicals. Free oxygen radicals are chemicals that are produced by the horse's body during the process of inflammation. They have been implicated in contributing to cell death and destruction. Therapy to remove these radicals is a relatively new avenue of treatment for inflammation.

In the horse, orgotein has been clinically tested for the treatment of traumatic arthritis, navicular disease and other limb and joint conditions. Response to the drug has been variable. It is supplied as a dehydrated powder that is mixed with sodium chloride solution prior to injection into the muscle.

When it was first tested, orgotein was injected into inflamed joints in an effort to control the inflammation. It was found that an unacceptable level of inflammation in the joint was produced by the injection of the drug itself. Recently the drug has been reintroduced for horses for intramuscular use only.

Orgotein appears to be extremely safe at doses far exceeding that recommended by the manufacturer.

PRECAUTIONS When orgotein is given to horses, inflammatory reactions sometimes appear to worsen prior to improving. Such signs are similar to the "joint flare" that is occasionally seen after medications are injected into joints. Treated areas may appear to become more inflamed with the onset of treatment; according to the manufacturer, treatment should not be stopped if such signs occur. Such signs must be differentiated from reinjury, however.

SIDE EFFECTS   Allergic reactions to orgotein have been reported. If signs of allergy are seen, treatment with the drug should be discontinued.

OXYQUINOLINE   *(8-Hydroxyquinoline)*

Oxyquinoline is a compound that helps control the growth of, but does not kill, bacteria and fungi. It can be used in the treatment of minor burns or scrapes. In horses, oxyquinoline is commonly available in a lanolin and petrolatum base and sold over the counter.

In man, oxyquinoline is available for the treatment of conditions such as athlete's foot and hemorrhoids.

OXYTOCIN

Oxytocin is a protein that is used in management of broodmares. It is available as a sterile solution that is generally given by intravenous injection. Oxytocin causes contraction of smooth muscle in the horse (smooth muscle is one of three different muscle types in the horse's body). In the mare, smooth muscle is found primarily in the uterus, the bladder and the gastrointestinal tract.

The mare's body normally produces oxytocin during the first stage of labor. Oxytocin release begins the process of contraction of the uterus, which ultimately results in the foal being pushed out of the mare's uterus. Oxytocin also stimulates the release of milk in lactating mares. Natural oxytocin release is stimulated by the foal bumping the mare's udder with its head and mouth.

The major clinical uses of oxytocin are in inducing labor in mares and in assisting removal of retained placentas. In addition, injections of oxytocin are used to help the uterus expel fluid after it has been treated by therapeutic lavage (rinsing with antibacterial solutions) and to help the uterus contract after birth or prolapse.

PRECAUTIONS   Oxytocin should be used with care if uterine bleeding has been identified. While oxytocin does help constrict uterine blood vessels, the muscle contraction induced by the drug may also cause pulling and tearing that could conceivably increase bleeding in some cases.

Some veterinarians have reported a higher incidence of fetal dystocias (where the fetus is delivered in an abnormal position) when labor is induced with oxytocin.

SIDE EFFECTS   Oxytocin causes contraction of all smooth muscle in the body. Accordingly, signs such as urination, colic and profuse sweating may accompany administration of oxytocin.

· P ·

PALOSEIN   (see Orgotein)

PANACUR   (see Benzimidazole)

PANALOG

Panalog is a proprietary name for a combination drug product made by Solvay Pharmaceuticals. It has been made for many years. It is widely used for the treatment of infectious and inflammatory conditions of the horse's skin and is also used by some practitioners to treat conditions of the ears and eyes.

Panalog contains antibacterial, antifungal and anti-inflammatory drugs. It is not specifically approved for use in the horse but is commonly used with no reported problems. Generic equivalents of this product are available.

PANTOTHENIC ACID *(D-Panthenol)*

Pantothenic acid is one of the group of water-soluble B-vitamins. There have been no dietary requirements for pantothenic acid recognized in the horse. Ample amounts of this vitamin are supplied in the normal horse diet and are produced by the intestinal bacteria. The exact function of pantothenic acid in the horse's body is not known.

Sterile solutions of D-panthenol are available for intravenous injection in the horse. Some veterinarians feel that it is a stimulant to normal movement of the intestines and use the vitamin as a treatment for colic. There is clinical evidence that suggests the vitamin doesn't have any effectiveness in this function.

PENICILLIN *Agri-Cillin, Crystacillin, Aquacillin*

Penicillin was the first antibiotic, discovered in 1928. It is actually a term for a class of drugs of which there are many members. In common usage, the term *penicillin* usually refers to the natural penicillin G, which is provided in sterile suspension for intramuscular injection.

Penicillin G is combined with procaine, a local anesthetic, to help take the sting out of the injection. Other types of penicillins do exist for intravenous injection; however, they are rarely used in the horse. Unlike in man, penicillin is reported to be poorly absorbed orally in the horse and causes diarrhea. Hence it is rarely given orally to the horse.

Penicillin G is the antibiotic of choice for the treatment of *Streptococcus* infections in the horse ("strangles"). As such, many misconceptions exist about its use. Penicillin G can be used to prevent the occurrence of strangles abscesses if therapy is instituted early enough in the disease. It has also been recommended that penicillin be given prophylactically to healthy horses in the face of an outbreak of strangles to keep them from getting the disease.

There is no evidence that the use of penicillin G causes or promotes the formation of abscesses inside the horse's body ("bastard strangles"). If a horse does have a strangles abscess forming and an inadequate dose of penicillin is given or if it is given for an insufficient period, the opening of the abscess to the outside of the body will tend to be delayed, however. Some veterinarians prefer to wait for strangles abscesses that form under the jaw to open and drain prior to instituting penicillin therapy.

Penicillin G is commonly used in association with aminoglycoside antibiotics for the treatment of severe infections of the horse. This combination increases the number of bacteria that are killed with antibiotic treatment.

Penicillin G is also available in combination with dihydrostreptomycin. This combination is rarely recommended in the horse, however. Bacterial resistance to dihydrostreptomycin occurs rapidly. In addition, the levels of penicillin G in this combination product are two-thirds of those found in procaine penicillin G alone. It has been said the combination combines an ineffective antibiotic with a reduced dose of an effective one. When penicillin therapy is considered, penicillin G alone is generally preferred to the combination product with dihydrostreptomycin.

Many penicillins have been chemically altered to increase their ability to kill bacteria. An example of such a drug is ampicillin sodium (see Ampicillin Sodium).

Benzethine penicillin is sometimes advocated as a longer-acting penicillin, that is, one that needs to be given less frequently than procaine penicillin. A number of products have been made to combine benzethine penicillin with the more commonly used procaine penicillin (Benza-Pen, Ambi-Pen, Dura-Pen, Flo-cillin, Twin-Pen, Pen BP-48). However, studies have shown no advantage to the use of this preparation over penicillin G alone. There appears to be no increased duration of effect with benzethine penicillin.

PRECAUTIONS   Care must be taken while giving penicillin G to ensure that it is given intramuscularly. If accidentally given intravenously, penicillin can knock a horse to the ground or even kill it. As with any injection intended to be given in the muscle, the syringe of penicillin should be aspirated (its plunger pulled back) prior to depressing the plunger. If blood is seen in the syringe, the needle should be withdrawn and the drug given elsewhere.

Injections of penicillin commonly cause muscle soreness or swelling at the site of injection. Most clinicians recommend that no more than 15 milliliters ("cc") of penicillin be given at any one injection site. This means that routinely recommended doses of the drug should be split into multiple injection sites to help avoid this complication.

Penicillin G cannot be used in show horses. The procaine that is added to the suspension of penicillin as an anesthetic cannot be differentiated from procaine or lidocaine that might be illegally used to desensitize a horse's lower limb (to keep him from limping, for example). If penicillin G therapy is used at a competition, the horse will test positive for the anesthetic.

SIDE EFFECTS   Generally, penicillins are quite safe. However, penicillin allergies are among the most commonly reported drug allergies in man. They are not commonly seen in horses, however. Of course, if a horse has an allergic response to penicillin, therapy with this drug should be stopped. Once an allergy to any of the penicillins is demonstrated, any type of penicillin therapy should be avoided in that horse.

PENTAZOCINE   *Talwin-V*

Pentazocine is a mild narcotic pain reliever that is occasionally used for relief of abdominal (colic) pain in the horse. Studies have shown it to be less effective at controlling pain than either xylazine or butorphanol.

Pentazocine is potentially addicting. It is a drug that is controlled by the U.S. Food and Drug Administration. Because it does not have profound pain-relieving effects and because of the problems inherent in keeping controlled substances, the use of pentazocine in horses has declined.

SIDE EFFECTS   At recommended doses, side effects such as sedation or sweating are not observed with pentazocine. At fifty percent above the recommended dose, however, incoordination is noted in some animals. Other side effects, such as marked incoordination and nervousness, are only noted when doses are exceeded by three to six times.

PEPTO-BISMOL   *(see Bismuth Compounds)*

PERNA CANALICULUS PREPARATION   *Synoflex, Arthroflex*

Perna canaliculus is a sea mussel. This mussel has high levels of glycosaminoglycans (GAGs) in it.

Glycosaminoglycans are important structural components of the body, especially the joints. According to the manufacturer, feeding perna mussel to horses is supposed to increase the level of GAGs in the joint, improving joint function and lubrication (see Polysulfated Glycosaminoglycan). There is no clinical evidence that feeding high levels of GAGs has any effect on the horse; however, anecdotal reports of the benefits of supplementation with perna mussel abound.

There are no reported adverse effects of perna mussel preparations. Some horses object to the smell of the supplement, however.

PETROLATUM   *Vaseline*

Petrolatum serves as the base for many of the ointments that are used on the skin of the horse and of man. Petrolatum also has some effect as an emollient and protectant for the skin. It is derived from hydrocarbons obtained from crude oil.

Petrolatum has no known therapeutic properties. It is highly occlusive to the skin; for this reason, it is an effective emollient (see Emollients).

For some reason, some people believe that applying petrolatum to a healing wound will help the wound grow hair. This idea is simply ridiculous.

PHENOL

Phenol is a synthetic chemical but can also be obtained from coal tar. It is also known as carbolic acid.

Phenol has a variety of pharmaceutical uses. It is a caustic agent and can be used to chemically cauterize wounds. It is a disinfectant that was commonly used years ago; other, more potent disinfectants have replaced phenol today. In dilute solutions, phenol is mildly anesthetic and is used to help control itching. Its most important use is probably as a preservative for injectable drugs.

In the horse, phenol is used in some over-the-counter hoof dressings, presumably for its disinfectant properties. Some liquid preparations rubbed on horse legs have also contained phenol because it is irritating to the skin (see Blister).

PHENYLBUTAZONE   *Equiphen, Butatron, Phen-Buta-Vet, Equipalazone, Pro-Bute*

Phenylbutazone ("bute") is without question the most commonly administered nonsteroidal anti-inflammatory pain-relieving drug for the horse. Time and use have demonstrated that phenylbutazone is very effective for the control of pain, inflammation and fever in the horse. It's also one of the least expensive drugs available for the horse. It comes in a one-gram tablet, a paste and a preground powder for oral administration to the horse as well as a sterile liquid for IV administration only (the drug is extremely irritating if injected in the muscle).

PRECAUTIONS   The use of phenylbutazone is carefully monitored by the AHSA. Horses exceeding allowable blood levels may be banned from future competitions.

Racing associations in many states do not allow the use of phenylbutazone.

SIDE EFFECTS   Phenylbutazone has been demonstrated to be a safe and effective pain reliever for the horse at recommended dosages. Its side effects are similar to aspirin and other nonsteroidal anti-inflammatory drugs (see Aspirin, Nonsteroidal Anti-Inflammatory Drug). For some reason, phenylbutazone does have something of an unwarranted reputation as being a dangerous drug in horses.

In certain circumstances, caution may be advisable in using phenylbutazone (or any of the related drugs). Two types of adverse side effects have been reported in the horse: gastrointestinal and renal (kidney). These effects are most commonly reported in foals and ponies; adverse effects are rarely reported in adult large-breed horses.

The reported gastrointestinal side effects of phenylbutazone are primarily ulcers. Ulcers are erosions of the surface of the mouth, stomach or intestines. This probably occurs as a result of some local effect of irritation from the drug when it is given orally. Ulcers are most commonly seen in foals that are maintained on phenylbutazone (or any other drug of the same class) for various conditions. Ulcers are rarely seen when phenylbutazone is given IV and then only at very high doses.

Kidney side effects are usually associated with decreased water consumption. In horses with kidney disease, illness occurs because of a failure of the kidneys to remove the body's waste products. The use of phenylbutazone should be carefully monitored in horses that are dehydrated, debilitated (and not drinking well) or that have disease of the kidneys. Care should be taken when using phenylbutazone in combination with other drugs that have side effects related to the kidney such as gentamycin or amikacin.

SIDE EFFECTS from the use phenylbutazone are extremely uncommon at the routinely prescribed doses. Doubling the recommended doses increases the potential for side effects, however. All drugs should be used according to your veterinarian's recommendations.

PHOSPHORUS

Phosphorus is a mineral required for normal development of the skeleton of the horse as well as for various metabolic functions. About eight percent of the horse's phosphorus is contained in the bones and teeth. Its levels in the body are closely associated with calcium levels. The horse's body tries to maintain a relatively constant ratio between the two minerals (see Calcium).

A deficiency of phosphorus produces problems with bone growth in young horses and softening of the bones in older ones. These changes are similar to those seen with calcium deficiencies.

An excess of phosphorus causes calcium absorption to be decreased by the horse's intestines. This condition was occasionally seen years ago but reports are rare now. The clinical disease was called "big head" or "bran disease" (it was seen in horses eating a diet consisting almost exclusively of wheat bran); the medical term for the disease is nutritional secondary hyperparathyroidism.

The dietary requirements for phosphorus are generally supplied in a normal horse's diet. However, some attention must be paid to the balance between calcium and phosphorus in the diet, especially in growing foals. Ratios from 1:1 (calcium level:phosphorus level) to 6:1 can be fed with no adverse effects on the growing horse as long as the absolute dietary requirements for phosphorus are met.

Alfalfa hay tends to have high levels of calcium relative to phosphorus. Grains tend to have higher phosphorus levels relative to calcium (see Calcium).

PINE OIL   *(Pine Needle Oil, Mentholated Syrup of White Pine)*

Pine oil comes from distilling various pine needles with steam. The oil is primarily used in perfume and as a flavoring agent.

In man, pine oil is also used in the treatment of bronchitis, where it is inhaled. In horses, pine oils are used in formulating some cough and liniment preparations. It would seem to have limited use for these purposes.

PINE TAR

Pine tar is obtained by distilling wood of certain species of pine trees. Its use was first reported in the early eighteenth century, when it was reported to cure literally every ailment known to man.

Pine tar has mild counterirritant and local antibacterial effects. It is most commonly applied to the hoof of the horse, particularly under horseshoe pads, in an effort to toughen the hoof or to control the growth of bacteria under the pad. It seems to work well enough in this regard.

PIPERAZINE

Piperazine is an antiparasitic agent that has been used since the 1950s. It kills relatively few internal parasites of the horse. Its actions are largely limited to ascarid infections, although it does have some effect on strongyles and pinworms. Ascarid infections can be important in foals and young horses.

Piperazine works by paralyzing or narcotizing the parasites, which are then swept out of the intestines by fecal material and the normal propulsive movements of the bowel.

Piperazine is also mixed with other deworming agents such as thiabendazole or trichlorfon (Equizole-A and Dyrex TF, respectively). The combination products increase the number of parasites killed when compared with piperazine alone.

PRECAUTIONS   Piperazine should not be used if extremely heavy ascarid infestations are suspected. The drug causes rapid death of the parasites in the intestines and intestinal blockages have occurred. Benzimidazole antiparasitic agents cause a slower, more prolonged death of the parasites and would be preferred in these circumstances.

SIDE EFFECTS   Piperazine is extremely safe at six to seven times the recommended dose and it can even be used on very young horses.

POLYMIXIN B   *Neosporin, Mycotracin, Neobacimyx, Panalog, Vetropolycin*

Polymixin B is an antibiotic with limited use in the horse. It kills relatively few bacteria; however, it is very effective in killing the bacteria that are sensitive to it. It is available in various ointments and can be obtained in pure liquid form.

Polymixin B is the antibiotic of choice for the treatment of infections caused by a bacteria called *Pseudomonas*. Infections by this bacteria most often occur in the eye or the uterus of the mare.

Polymixin B is frequently combined with bacitracin and neomycin, other antibiotics that increase the number of bacteria killed compared to each antibiotic alone (see Bacitracin, Neomycin). It is also frequently combined with corticosteroid anti-inflammatory agents (see Corticosteroid).

POLYSULFATED GLYCOSAMINOGLYCAN *(PSGAG) Adequan*

Polysulfated glycosaminoglycan is chemically similar to substances that occur in normal joint cartilage (mucopolysaccharides). Two preparations of PSGAG are available for the horse. Both are sterile solutions. One solution is injected directly into joints and the other is given IM.

PSGAG inhibits enzymes that are released during joint inflammation. Inflammatory enzymes break down and degrade joint cartilage, which ultimately impairs joint function. Through this anti-inflammatory effect, some protection is provided the cartilage, and joint function is ultimately improved. Experimentally, when horse knee joints that have been inflamed by injecting a chemical into them are treated with PSGAG, protein levels in inflamed joints are reduced and the thickness (viscosity) of the joint fluid is increased. In the laboratory, PSGAG causes increased production of hyaluronic acid by the lining cells of the joint membrane (synovial cells). It may also stimulate the synthesis of glycosaminoglycans by cartilage cells themselves.

PSGAG has been evaluated extensively but its actual effects in the horse are still relatively poorly understood. Unfortunately, for all of the good things that can be observed in the laboratory, the clinical benefits of PSGAG are more difficult to measure. PSGAG does appear to be an excellent anti-inflammatory drug when it is injected into joints that have been treated with a chemical to cause inflammation. However, PSGAG has not shown any obvious beneficial effects on healing when it is injected into joints in which there have been surgically created defects in the cartilage.

It seems clear that PSGAG does have some good effects as an anti-inflammatory agent for joints when it is injected directly into them. Whether such effects are more than just anti-inflammatory (i.e., protective of the joint cartilage) has not been demonstrated in the horse.

The effects of injection of PSGAG into muscle are even less clear. It is likely that PSGAG does reach concentrations in horse joints when it is injected into the muscle. It is probable that it exerts some anti-inflammatory effect and that multiple joints may be affected by a single IM injection. However, it is also likely that the effect on a particular joint will be less than if PSGAG is given directly into that joint. It is unlikely, however, that PSGAG given into the muscle has any significant effect on delaying the development of or helping in the repair of damaged, arthritic joints.

PSGAG is also becoming a popular drug for the treatment of acute tendon injury and inflammation. Its use has been described both injected in the muscle and injected directly into the tendon for this purpose.

PRECAUTIONS   Like all injections into joints, routine precautions should be followed when using PSGAG, such as clipping the hair over the joint, scrubbing the skin surface with antiseptics and wearing protective latex gloves.

SIDE EFFECTS   Injections of PSGAG into horse joints have been associated with inflammatory joint reactions, similar to allergic reactions in the joint. These usually are self-limiting. They must be differentiated from joint infections, which are much more serious.

PSGAG injections may also increase the potential for bacteria to cause joint infections, should bacteria be introduced into the joint by the injection process.

There are no known side effects or reactions that have been reported with the IM use of PSGAG.

POTASSIUM IODIDE

Potassium iodide is a chemical that is used in a variety of medications and preparations for the horse. Its chief use is as an expectorant that helps liquify thick mucus in respiratory diseases. It can also be applied to the skin, where it has mild antifungal properties.

An old treatment for thrush, an infection of the horse's foot, involves applying potassium iodide to the foot and then pouring on liquid turpentine. The resulting purple smoke is quite dramatic and the treatment does kill bacteria in the foot. This application of potassium iodide can burn the skin of the lower limb, so it should be used carefully, if at all.

POULTICE   *Numotizine, Up-Tite, Animalintex*

Poultices are moist substances that are commonly applied to the limbs and hooves of the horse. They are typically made up of clay or other earthen materials mixed with many other substances such as glycerin, kaolin, boric acid, aloe vera and oils of such things as peppermint and wintergreen.

Poultices are commonly used in an effort to help reduce limb swelling or foot soreness in horses. As the agents dry, it is possible that they tend to dehydrate the surface tissue or absorb surface fluid into them. The actual medical benefits of poultices are unknown.

Poultices almost certainly do not "draw out" tissue infections such as abscesses. How such an effect would be possible is difficult to imagine because poultices do not penetrate tissue. Tissue is not permeable by poultice, which is good, since absorption of clay or other earthen materials into the circulation would presumably be very bad for the horse's health. Also, since no substance can freely move back and forth across body tissue, an osmotic effect on abscesses should not be possible. Poultices should not be able to bring fluid underneath the skin to the surface.

In human medicine, poultices are generally warm, moist mixtures of such things as hot water and linseed meal. These are frequently applied between layers of cloth or muslin. The purpose of a poultice is to keep the treated areas hot and moist. In this manner, poultices increase tissue heat but may cause some local skin irritation. Interestingly, warm applications of poultice are rarely used in the horse. Cold commercially made poultice preparations are those that seem to be most frequently used in horses.

POVIDONE-IODINE   *Betadine, Prodine, Vetadine*

Povidone-iodine solutions and soaps are almost certainly the antiseptic agents most frequently used in the horse. Povidone is a dispersing and suspending agent that, when heated with iodine, forms a compound that has about ten percent of undiluted iodine activity.

Povidone-iodine compound is therefore often referred to as "tamed" iodine. Povidone-iodine has all of the beneficial antiseptic effects of iodine but virtually none of the undesirable qualities, such as tissue irritation and staining.

Povidone-iodine preparations are useful in removing germs from the skin for the treatment of skin diseases, for cleansing prior to surgical and injection procedures and for wound care. It can also be used for disinfection of stalls and equipment. Povidone-iodine is available in solutions, solution-containing soaps and in ointments.

Frequent use of povidone-iodine shampoos is reported to cause drying of the hair coat in horses. They can also be irritating to human skin.

PREDNISONE/PREDNISOLONE

Prednisone and prednisolone are short-acting corticosteroids. The drugs are available in pills for oral administration to the horse and are effective when used as directed (see Corticosteroid). A liquid preparation of prednisone is available in drops to control inflammation of the eye.

PROGESTERONE

Progesterone or progestins are most commonly given to mares. These drugs have many applications for controlling the reproductive cycle of the mare. Uses include: (1) regulation of estrus ("heat") in mares undergoing transition from their inactive to active breeding periods; (2) synchronization of estrus in cycling mares; (3) delaying estrus and ovulation in mares after they have foaled; (4) long-term suppression of the signs of estrus and (5) maintenance of pregnancy in mares that tend to lose their fetuses early in pregnancy.

It should be noted that although it is commonly done, there is little clinical data to indicate that giving supplemental progesterone is effective in maintaining pregnancy in problem mares that tend to abort their fetuses early in term. In normal mares that are in foal, the placenta takes over production of progesterone from the ovaries at about day one hundred to one hundred twenty of pregnancy. If supplementation of progesterone is desired, there is no certainly no reason to continue it past this time.

PROGESTERONE "IMPLANTS"

In show and race mares, suppression of the signs of estrus is frequently requested. Daily administration of altrenogest appears to be effective in suppressing estrus for long periods and does not affect subsequent fertility (see Altrenogest). Intermittent intravenous injections of progesterone in an oil base may also be used for estrus supression. However, in an effort to avoid frequent drug administration, the use of other, longer-acting progestins has been attempted.

"Implants" of progesterone are one method that is advocated by some veterinarians. These are reported to provide a slow, continuous release of progestin from a pellet implanted under the skin of the mare.

It should be noted that there are no implants made from progestins that have been designed or approved for use in horses. Among the implants that are used are norgestomet (Synchro-mate B), a growth promoter used in feedlot cattle. A number of studies have found norgestomet to be ineffective in suppressing estrus or estrus behavior in the mare, even when given in daily doses. Other progesterone-containing cattle implants are also used in horses. Their effectiveness and safety in horses is unknown and has never been evaluated.

PROMAZINE HYDROCHLORIDE   *Promazine Granules,*
Tranquazine Injection

Promazine hydrochloride is a tranquilizing agent from the same class of drugs as acepromazine. It is available in granules for oral administration or as a liquid for IV administration for the horse. It is indicated for a variety of procedures in which a calmer horse is desired, such as shoeing, dental care or in handling mares during breeding.

Promazine seems to be somewhat inconsistent in its effects. Some horses show little if any tranquilization after dosage with promazine. The manufacturer of the IV product suggests that a short period of quiet for the horse prior to administration of the drug may encourage a more favorable response.

PRECAUTIONS   Routine precautions should be followed in working around a horse that is tranquilized. Horses under tranquilization can still react quickly to external stimuli.

Promazine hydrochloride should be used with care in horses showing signs of illness or shock. Promazine should not be used in conjuction with organophosphate compounds because it increases their toxicity. If used with procaine, promazine increases procaine's activity.

The use of promazine is strictly prohibited in horses showing under the rules of the AHSA.

SIDE EFFECTS   As with acepromazine, paralysis of the muscles that retract the penis has been associated with promazine hydrochloride. The cause of this side effect is not known but it is, fortunately, quite rare (see Acepromazine).

PROPYLENE GLYCOL

Propylene glycol is a solvent and preservative used to mix various drugs and over-the-counter preparations. It is also used in the manufacture of ointment bases.

Propylene glycol has no known therapeutic activity. Many drugs are mixed with propylene glycol in the manufacture of pharmacologic products.

PROPYLPARABEN

Propylparaben is a preservative agent with antifungal properties. It is used to help preserve cosmetic preparations that contain fats and oils.

Propylparaben is used as a preservative in a variety of hoof dressings for horses. Hoof dressings contain high quantities of various oils (see Hoof Dressings).

PROSTAGLANDIN

Prostaglandins are a group of compounds with a remarkable spectrum of biological activity. Their biological effects are believed to cover almost every activity of the body. Altering prostaglandin synthesis is the method by which the most commonly used nonsteroidal anti-inflammatory drugs work (see Nonsteroidal Anti-Inflammatory Drug). Synthetic derivatives of prostaglandin are also commonly used in management of the reproductive cycle of the mare (see Prostaglandins and the Reproductive Cycle of the Mare).

PROSTAGLANDINS AND THE REPRODUCTIVE CYCLE OF THE MARE *Lutalyse, Equimate*

Prostaglandins are widely used for control of the mare's reproductive cycle. Synthetic forms of the hormone are used to break down (lyse) a structure on the mare's ovary known as the corpus luteum. These drugs are provided as sterile solutions that are most commonly given IM in the mare.

During the mare's estrus (heat) cycle, her ovary produces the egg from a structure called a follicle. After the follicle releases the egg, the follicle transforms into a hormone-producing structure called the corpus luteum. The corpus luteum is responsible for the production of progesterone, the hormone that keeps mares out of heat. Progesterone is also the hormone that maintains pregnancy (see Progesterone).

Prostaglandin is normally released by the mare's body when it is time for her to come back into heat. Prostaglandin causes the corpus luteum to break down. Consequently, progesterone production decreases and she will again demonstrate signs of heat.

Giving prostaglandins to the mare mimics the natural process. However, for injectable prostaglandins to be effective, the corpus luteum must be mature. Therefore, the drug will not work properly until at least four or five days after the last day of the mare's heat cycle.

The uses of injectable prostaglandin therefore all depend on its abilities to break down the corpus luteum. Among these uses are: (1) to end situations where the corpus luteum persists; (2) to shorten the interval between heat cycles and allow for earlier rebreeding; (3) to try to control the time of ovulation; (4) to help treat uterine infections by inducing heat and (5) to abort the fetus early in the pregnancy.

PRECAUTIONS   Prostaglandins can be absorbed through human skin and could cause abortion or bronchial spasms in people. Pregnant women and asthmatics should handle it carefully. If it gets on the skin, it should be washed off immediately with soap and water.

Prostaglandins should not be used at the same time as nonsteroidal anti-inflammatory drugs. Nonsteroidal anti-inflammatory drugs block the effects of prostaglandins. They should also not be given to horses suffering from gastrointestinal or respiratory problems.

SIDE EFFECTS   After horses have been given prostaglandin, sweating, mild diarrhea and colic signs have been observed. These signs are usually transient and disappear within an hour. Clinical experience suggests that these signs are seen more frequently with dinoprost than with fluprostenol or other synthetic prostaglandins.

PROTEIN

Proteins are the basic building blocks from which tissue is made. Proteins also make up some of the hormones and all of the enzymes of the horse's body. Eighty percent of the horse's structure is protein (after the fat and water are removed). Protein is constantly being used by the horse. Even though the horse's body reuses some of its own protein, a steady supply must be available in the diet to replace some of what is lost or used up.

Growing horses are more sensitive to protein needs than are adult horses. If protein is restricted in the diet in foals, growth is restricted as well. In adult horses, inadequate protein can cause decreased appetite, loss of body tissue and poor hoof growth and hair coat.

Excessive protein intake by horses appears to cause no obvious harm. However, there are studies that suggest that excessive protein intake may be associated with decreased performance. Exercising horses do not require supplemental protein.

Extra protein does not make a horse stronger. Protein is needed for growth of tissue but extra protein does not cause extra strength or muscle growth. Extra protein is merely burned as fuel or converted to fat. Digesting protein requires much work by the horse's body and giving a horse excessive amounts of protein is just an expensive and inefficient way to give him extra calories.

Most horse diets supply more than ample amounts of protein. Additional protein may be needed by horses for growth and lactation if these horses are fed some grass or poor-quality hays. However, alfalfa-based rations generally supply plenty of protein for horses of all ages and metabolic requirements.

PSYLLIUM   *(Hydrophyllic Mucilloid)* **Sand-Lax, Equi-Lax, Metamucil**

Psyllium is made from the outer portion of psyllium seeds. Psyllium attracts large amounts of water to it and therefore has some effect as a stool softener.

In horses, psyllium has been demonstrated to be about the only substance that is effective in removing accumulations of sand from the intestine. Horses can inadvertently eat sand when they pull hay or grass from the ground when they are fed in areas of sandy soil. It has also been recommended as a treatment for some types of impaction colics (constipation).

It is recommended that horses not be fed psyllium for more than three consecutive weeks. Feeding psyllium for longer periods than this is not harmful, but if psyllium is provided to the horse constantly, the horse's intestinal tract may begin to digest it and thus render it ineffective.

PYRANTEL   *Strongid, Imathal*

Pyrantel is an antiparasitic agent commonly used in the horse. It comes in a paste for oral administration, a liquid for administration via nasogastric intubation (stomach tube) and a pelleted formulation that is given daily in the feed. Pyrantel causes paralysis of intestinal parasites. The parasites are then removed from the body by normal intestinal movements.

Pyrantel is effective for control of the majority of equine intestinal parasites, with the exception of bots. Pyrantel is the only deworming agent that has demonstrated effectiveness against the equine tapeworm; the dose must be doubled to achieve this effect.

SIDE EFFECTS   Pyrantel is considered safe for all horses at up to twenty times overdose.

PYRILAMINE MALEATE

Pyrilamine is an antihistamine for use in the horse. It comes as a sterile solution and is given by IM or IV injection (see Antihistamine).

PYRIMETHAMINE   *Daraprim*

Pyrimethamine is used for the treatment of equine protozoal myeloencephalitis, a protozoal infection of the spinal cord of the horse. For the treatment of this condition, pyrimethamine is used along with a sulfa-trimethoprim combination antibacterial drug (see Sulfamethoxazole-Trimethoprim). Treatment for protozoal myeloencephalitis must frequently be continued for several months. Pyrimethamine comes as a tablet for oral administration to the horse.

SIDE EFFECTS   No adverse side effects of pyrimethamine have been reported in the horse.

· R ·

RANITIDINE   *Zantac*

Ranitidine is an antihistamine that is used for the treatment of stomach ulcers in the horse. Its effects are similar to those of cimetidine (see Cimetidine). Ranitidine is a newer drug than cimetidine. It is available in pill form for oral administration.

REGUMATE   *(see Altrenogest)*

RHEAFORM   *(see Clioquinol)*

RIBOFLAVIN   *(see Vitamin B-2)*

RIFAMPIN

Rifampin is an antibiotic used most commonly in the treatment of pneumonias in foals caused by *Rhodococcus equi.* It is available as a pill for oral administration.

Rifampin is almost always given in combination with erythromy-cin. The two drugs given together increase the effectiveness over what is seen when each drug is given alone (see Erythromycin).

PRECAUTIONS   Bacterial resistance to rifampin alone occurs rap-idly. That's why it is almost always given in combination with other drugs.

SIDE EFFECTS   Softening of the stool can be seen in foals treated with rifampin. While this usually does not mean that treatment should be stopped, foals with soft stools as a result of this treatment should be monitored closely. Sometimes severe diarrhea develops in treated foals, in which case the drug must be discontinued.

Rifampin can also cause reddish discoloration of the foal's urine.

RINTAL   *(see Febantel)*

ROBAXIN   *(see Methocarbamol)*

ROMPUN   *(see Xylazine)*

ROSEMARY OIL

Rosemary oil is distilled from rosemary flowers. It is a component of a popular liniment/bathing agent for the horse. It is also used as a flavoring agent and perfume.

· S ·

SALICYLIC ACID

Salicylic acid is chemically related to aspirin. However, it cannot be used internally because it is very irritating to the intestinal tract. Rather, it is applied to the skin, where it has a slight antiseptic action. Salicylic acid also tends to loosen and break down the surface layers of the skin; for that reason it is often used in the treatment of warts and corns in man.

In horses, salicylic acid is a component of various liniment and poultice preparations that are sold over the counter.

SALINE SOLUTION

Saline solution is a solution of sodium chloride (the chemical that is the primary component of table salt) in water. It is generally mixed so that it has the same concentration of salts as is present in body fluids (tonicity). It is the primary component of most over-the-counter preparations for use in the eye. Concentrated saline ointments are available for use in helping reduce swelling of the cornea of the eye; these are available by prescription only.

Saline solution is used in equine veterinary medicine mostly to mix and dilute injectable drugs. Undiluted, it can be given intravenously; it is the fluid of choice for the treatment of foals with ruptured bladders. For treatment of other conditions requiring intravenous fluids, other solutions that are less acidic than saline solution are more commonly used.

SARAPIN

Sarapin is a vegetable-based pain relieving agent for the horse. It comes in a sterile solution. It is most commonly given by injection into muscles or along peripheral nerves.

Little information about sarapin is available in veterinary literature. It is most commonly used in injections along the horse's back to relieve back spasms and in injections along the nerves running to the heel of the horse's foot in attempt to temporarily relieve heel soreness.

There are no reports of adverse effects to sarapin.

PRECAUTIONS   Sarapin can be detected in drug screening tests conducted by the AHSA.

SASSAFRAS OIL

Sassafras oil is an aromatic oil obtained from the sassafras tree. It is a flavoring agent used to make hard candies. It is also a preservative and has mild antiseptic properties. It can be used, along with other agents, for treatment of diseases of the nose and throat.

Sassafras oil is used to make pleasant-smelling solutions for bathing the horse.

SCARLET OIL

Scarlet oil is not a specific product. Rather, it is a combination of substances mixed together and dyed with Biebrich scarlet red, a chemical dye that gives it the characteristic color. Scarlet oil is an over-the-counter preparation for treatment of wounds.

Substances contained in various scarlet oil preparations include mineral oil, isopropyl alcohol, pine oil, benzyl alcohol, eucalyptus oil, methyl salicylate, and phenol (see various individual headings; Wound Treatments). The application of scarlet oil is recommended by some veterinarians to help promote the growth of granulation tissue. The ingredients in the mixture would seem to have little actual benefit in wound treatment.

SELENIUM

Selenium is a trace mineral that, among other things, functions as an antioxidant in the body. Antioxidant compounds prevent or delay the deterioration of substances when they are exposed to oxygen.

Selenium activity is apparently most important for normal muscle function. In the horse's body, it works in close association with vitamin E.

Selenium is commonly combined with vitamin E in preparations advocated for treatment of exertional rhabdomyolysis (myositis or "tying up"). Exactly what effect this combination of vitamin and mineral is supposed to have on this condition is unclear. Experimental evidence for the effectiveness of this combination at preventing rhabdomyolysis is lacking.

Selenium deficiencies are reported to occur in areas where the soil is lacking in selenium, particularly in some areas of the Great Lakes region and the Eastern, Gulf and Northwestern coasts. Selenium deficiency is commonly referred to as "white muscle disease." It occurs mostly in young foals whose mothers have received inadequate levels of the mineral. Affected foals have marked muscle weakness and listlessness as the principal signs of their disease.

Selenium toxicity is also seen, primarily in areas such as the Rocky Mountains or Great Plains, where selenium levels in the ground are high. Plants can accumulate high levels of selenium in these areas. Signs of toxicity include lameness that is often confused with laminitis, rough and brittle hair coat and swelling of the coronary band.

SHARK CARTILAGE

Shark cartilage supplements are the latest in a seemingly unending stream of products that are purportedly beneficial for the treatment of arthritis. There are no studies on the use of shark cartilage in horses. It is likely that shark cartilage, like all cartilage, has high levels of glycosaminoglycans. If this is so and if they are absorbed by the horse's large intestines, the theoretical benefits might be similar to those obtained with similar products (see Chondroitin Sulfate, Perna

Canaliculus Preparation, Polysulfated Glycosaminoglycan). Note the frequent use of the word *if* in this paragraph.

SODIUM BICARBONATE   *(Bicarbonate of Soda)*

Sodium bicarbonate (baking soda) is available as a white powder for oral administration or in sterile solution for IV administration for the horse. It has two main uses.

In solution, sodium bicarbonate may be used in the treatment of systemic acidosis in the horse by some veterinarians. Such conditions may occur during various types of shock.

Oral solutions of sodium bicarbonate ("milkshakes") have been given to horses *prior* to exercise in an effort to help their blood remove acid produced during exercise. This would theoretically increase endurance and performance, particularly in racing animals. This treatment can be dangerous. Not only that, but bicarbonate has been shown to be largely ineffective in increasing endurance or performance in experimental situations in racehorses. "Jugging" with bicarbonate solutions is prohibited by many racing organizations.

The use of sodium bicarbonate "milkshakes" in endurance horses is absolutely harmful. Sweating endurance horses actually tend to become *less* acidic (alkalosis) as they exercise. Giving these horses bicarbonate before exercise would tend to make their metabolic problems worse.

Sodium bicarbonate is sometimes fed to the horse in efforts to prevent exertional rhabdomyolysis (myositis or "tying up"). There is one clinical report in the veterinary literature of this treatment being effective in one mare that tied up frequently. However, horses may choose not to eat large amounts of sodium bicarbonate.

SODIUM BORATE

Sodium borate has some usefulness as an anti-itch agent when it is applied to the skin. It is used to help make various preparations of cosmetic ointments and lotions. Dilute sodium borate solutions have been used to make a rinse for the eye. Sodium borate has very limited therapeutic properties.

Sodium borate is a component of a hoof dressing and a coolant gel used on the horse's leg. Its purpose in these preparations is not apparent.

SORBITOL

Sorbitol is an alcohol that is most commonly used as a flavoring agent. It tastes sweet. Sorbitol has some mild effects as a laxative and moisturizer; it is found in an over-the-counter preparation for coughing in the horse. It has no known effects against coughing.

SPEARMINT OIL

Spearmint oil is derived from the spearmint plant. It is an aromatic oil that is used as a flavoring agent. It is also used in the manufacture of an over-the-counter "brace." Spearmint oil has no known therapeutic value but it smells great.

STANOZOLOL   *Winstrol-V*

Stanozolol is an anabolic steroid for use as an aid in treating debilitated horses. The drug is used in an effort to promote appetite, weight gain and the general physical condition of the horse and to help speed up recovery from disease. It comes as a sterile suspension for intramuscular administration in the horse. Injection in the gluteal muscles is recommended by the manufacturer.

PRECAUTIONS   Anabolic steroids have the potential to cause stallion-like behavior in the horse. These effects are reported to be lower in horses receiving stanozolol than in those receiving other similar drugs (see Boldenone Undecylenate). The longer that the horse is kept on the drug and the higher the dosage, however, the more likely this complication is to be seen.

There is no data on the effects of stanozolol on stallions, pregnant mares or fetuses. The effects of other androgenic steroids have been studied in mares and it has been determined that they interrupt normal reproductive function, although normal reproductive function does eventually return once the drug is withdrawn. However, depending on the dose, normal reproductive function may take many months, or even years, to return. For that reason, use of stanozolol in mares intended for breeding should probably be avoided.

SIDE EFFECTS   Because stanozolol causes retention of water and sodium, care should be used in giving this drug to horses with heart or kidney problems (see Anabolic Steroid).

STEARIC ACID

Stearic acid is a solidifying agent used in the preparation of many creams and ointments. There are many compounds that are derived from stearic acid; the letters *stear* in the chemical name of an ingredient denote its presence in a product. All stearic acid compounds are used for the same thing, as an ointment base.

In horses, stearic acid and its various derivatives are used frequently in preparing hoof dressings.

STEROID

Steroid is a term that refers to a chemical configuration that is shared by all drugs of this class. In common usage, the term has become

almost meaningless and is frequently used in a negative manner because of widespread abuses of these types of drugs as well as their
considerable side effects.

A number of drugs are considered steroids. These include:
(1) androgenic or anabolic steroids (see Anabolic Steroid); (2) anti-
inflammatory agents (see Corticosteroid) and (3) progesterone and
other female sex hormones (see Progesterone).

STRONGID   (see Pyrantel)

SUCRALFATE   Carafate

Sucralfate is a complex polysaccharide (sugar) that is used in the treatment of stomach ulcers in the horse. It comes as a tablet for oral
administration.

As sucralfate dissolves, the sugars apparently form a protective
coating over an ulcer. Healing of the ulcer evidently proceeds nicely
under this coating.

SULFA

Sulfa is a general term for a group of antibacterial agents with wide use
in medicine. The most commonly used sulfa drugs in the horse are
sulfamethoxazole and sulfadiazine. The drugs are frequently combined
with trimethoprim to increase their effectiveness.

Sulfa drugs are commonly given orally but are also used topically,
for treatments of wounds and infections. Intravenous preparations of sulfa are also used by some veterinarians. An intravenous
preparation of sulfadiazine and trimethoprim was available previously, but it was withdrawn because of numerous reports of adverse
reactions.

SULFAMETHOXAZOLE-TRIMETHOPRIM   *(SMZ-TMP)*

Sulfamethoxazole-trimethoprim (SMZ-TMP) is an antibacterial combination used in the treatment of a variety of infectious conditions in the horse. SMZ-TMP comes in pill form for oral administration.

Combining the two drugs increases (potentiates) the effectiveness of each drug. Because the combination of drugs is relatively inexpensive and is given orally, it is popularly used in the treatment of many different types of infections of the horse.

PRECAUTIONS   SMZ-TMP should not be used in horses that have exercise-induced pulmonary hemorrhage ("bleeders"). The drugs can potentially increase bleeding during exercise. The drug should be used with care in immature foals.

SIDE EFFECTS   Allergic reactions to SMZ-TMP are apparently rare in the horse but are reported in other species.

SULFUR

Sulfur is one of the basic elements in nature. It is needed in extremely small amounts in the horse's diet. Neither deficiencies nor toxicities of sulfur have ever been reported in the horse. Sulfur-containing supplements available for horses include methionine and methylsulfonylmethane (see Methionine, Methylsulfonylmethane).

Sulfur is also a component of various ointments, creams, shampoos and powders applied to the skin of the horse. Here, sulfur is used because it kills bacteria, kills fungus and helps remove surface skin cells.

SULFURIC ACID

Sulfuric acid is a caustic chemical that is used in various industrial processes such as etching metal. It has no known pharmaceutical value.

Sulfuric acid is a component of an over-the-counter wound dressing available for horses (see Wound Dressings). Sulfuric acid is not something that would normally be considered good for a wound.

SUPEROXIDE DISMUTASE

Superoxide dismutase is one of a group of substances that scavenge (pick up and remove) free oxygen radicals. Free oxygen radicals are byproducts of the process of inflammation. They can cause severe tissue damage. Obviously, something that could remove these radicals from the system would be of great benefit. Superoxide dismutase therapy is relatively new and its uses and effectiveness are poorly understood.

Superoxide dismutase preparations have been advertised for oral administration in the horse. Their effectiveness is unknown, however, and no studies are available to support the beneficial claims made for these products. In fact, it's unlikely that superoxide dismutase, a protein, can make it through the digestive process intact. A pharmaceutical preparation for intramuscular administration is available in the horse (see Orgotein).

SWEAT WRAP

Sweat wrap describes a method of applying something to the horse's limb. A medication is placed on the limb and then covered with a plastic wrap; then the leg is bandaged. The lack of air to the leg causes it to build up heat and to "sweat."

After "sweating" the leg, moisture will accumulate on the leg. After the wrap is removed, frequently the skin will appear to be "tighter." Sweat wraps do not "drive" medication through the layers of the skin; that isn't possible.

The effectiveness of sweat wraps appears to be directly related to how serious the underlying problem is. They do seem to be able to help reduce minor accumulations of fluid that occur under the skin of the horse's limb. They do not seem to be effective at treating injuries of deeper structures.

A number of medications are used to formulate sweat wraps, including nitrofurazone ointment, glycerin, DMSO and corticosteroids.

· T ·

TAGAMET *(see Cimetidine)*

TALWIN *(see Pentazocine)*

TANNIC ACID

Tannic acid is an astringent agent, produced from various species of oak tree (see Astringent).

Tannic acid was a compound that found much use in medicine in the past. When taken internally, it was used as a treatment for diarrhea. Applied externally, tannic acid was used as a treatment for burns. When applied to burns, tannic acid causes a hard covering to form, by virtue of its astringent action. It fell out of favor as a burn treatment when it was found that tannic acid did not kill bacteria and actually promoted the death of healthy tissue, effects that are obviously undesirable. Tannic acid has also been used for the treatment of bedsores in man.

Tannic acid is a component of an over-the-counter preparation sold for the treatment of wounds in the horse. Its caustic effects would seem to make it a poor choice for treatment of wounds.

TBZ   *(Thiabendazole; see Benzimidazole)*

TELMIN   *(Mebendazole; see Benzimidazole)*

TETRACYCLINE   *(Oxytetracycline) LA-200, Bio-Mycin, Terramycin, Oxyject 100, Medamycin*

Tetracyclines are a group of antibiotics that are not commonly used in the horse. Tetracyclines do kill a wide variety of bacteria. Oxytetracycline, the most widely used form of tetracycline, is supplied as a sterile liquid for IV or IM administration in the horse. The IM route is not commonly used, however, because it tends to make horses' muscles sore at the site of injection.

Tetracycline injections are generally selected in two specific circumstances. They are the drug of choice for the treatment of Potomac horse fever (equine monocytic ehrlichiosis), a disease characterized by fever, depression and diarrhea.

Tetracyclines are also administered to foals with tendon contractures early in life. Some foals will be observed to develop limb deformities early in life characterized by knuckling over at the fetlock joint or standing on the toes. Tetracycline is used here for its ability to bind calcium; this causes muscle and tendon relaxation. After large doses of tetracyclines, contracted tendons are frequently observed to relax in affected foals.

Tetracyclines are also available in ophthalmic preparations that are sold over the counter for the treatment of eye infections.

PRECAUTIONS   When given intravenously, rapid administration of tetracycline has caused animals to collapse. This is because it rapidly binds up body calcium, which is needed for normal muscle function, including heart muscle activity. This same effect is not seen when the drug is given slowly.

SIDE EFFECTS   Tetracycline is relatively nontoxic. Some veterinarians are reluctant to use tetracycline in the horse, however, because of a report in 1973 that the drug caused colitis (inflammation of the colon) and severe diarrhea in the horse. As the use of the drug has become more widespread recently, especially for the treatment of Potomac horse fever and tendon contractures, this complication has not commonly been reported. It may be that tetracycline is much safer than was once thought.

THIAMINE   *(see Vitamin B-1)*

THYME

Thyme is a cooking herb. It has some internal applications in herbal medicine for things such as asthma and headache. Its external use is not reported.

Thyme is found in a liniment preparation sold over the counter for horses (see Liniment). It is presumably a flavoring agent in this preparation.

THYMOL

Thymol is obtained from a plant oil by distillation. In horses, thymol is used in liniment preparations. It has some use as an anti-bacterial and antifungal agent; however, there are many more effective agents. It has a thymelike odor that is not unpleasant. This may also be one of the reasons that it is added to horse preparations.

TORBUGESIC   *(see Butorphanol)*

TRACE MINERALS

Trace minerals are inorganic substances that are required in very small amounts (hence the term *trace*) by the body. They exist in interrelationships that are very complex and poorly understood.

Many trace minerals are of biological importance to the animal. As a practical matter, such small amounts of these minerals are necessary that it is virtually impossible to create a diet that is lacking in them. Even when deficiencies exist, sometimes there are no clinical signs to demonstrate that fact. Some of these elements (for example, aluminum) can be demonstrated to exist in horse tissue but have no known function.

While undoubtedly important in some manner to the body, conditions where specific deficiencies of trace minerals exist are unknown in the horse. Conversely, conditions where toxicities occur as a result of oversupplementation are not reported either.

TRIAMCINOLONE   *Vetalog*

Triamcinolone is a corticosteroid anti-inflammatory agent used in the horse (see Corticosteroid). It is considered a long-lasting corticosteroid.

A variety of preparations of triamcinolone are available for the horse. It comes as a powder for oral administration or as a liquid for IM, IV, intra-articular or intralesional administration. It also makes up a number of products that are applied to the skin, either directly or in combination with other drugs (see Panalog).

PRECAUTIONS   Prior to an injection into the joint, routine procedures for cleanliness, such as clipping and scrubbing the joint and the use of latex gloves, should be followed to help decrease the chances of joint infection.

Transient inflammatory reactions ("joint flare") may be seen after injections into joints. This will usually subside in twenty-four to forty-eight hours but must be distinguished from joint infections.

As with all corticosteroids, caution should be used in giving triamcinolone in the last trimester of pregnancy due to the possibility of induction of premature labor.

SIDE EFFECTS   The systemic use of corticosteroid agents such as triamcinolone is reported to occasionally cause laminitis in some horses. The reason for this side effect is unknown. Longer-acting agents such as triamcinolone are considered to be more likely to cause this effect than are shorter-acting corticosteroids.

TRICHLORFON   *ComBot, Neguvon*

Trichlorfon is an antiparasitic agent for the horse. It is available in a paste formulation for oral administration or a liquid formulation for administration via nasogastric intubation (stomach tube).

Trichlorfon is frequently combined with other parasiticides, generally benzimidazoles, to increase the number of parasites that are killed by a single dose. In particular, trichlorfon is added to the benzimidazole drugs because of its ability to kill stomach bots. It kills parasites by interfering with their nervous system transmission, effectively paralyzing them and allowing for their removal by the horse's intestines.

PRECAUTIONS   Horses should be given trichlorfon after feeding to help reduce incidences of colic and diarrhea. It should not be used in horses during the last month of pregnancy because it can potentially cause mares to go into premature labor.

SIDE EFFECTS   Trichlorfon does not have a wide margin of safety in the horse, unlike other parasiticides. At two to four times the recommended dosage, it can cause colic and diarrhea. Other side effects associated with the nervous system, such as anxiety and incoordination, have been reported, occasionally even at normal doses.

Because of the potential for side effects and the relatively limited numbers of parasites killed by trichlorfon, its use has been greatly reduced. Its function as a boticide has been largely taken over by ivermectin (see Ivermectin).

TRYPTOPHAN   *(L-tryptophan)*

Tryptophan is an amino acid that has been promoted as a "natural" tranquilizing agent. Tryptophan is found in high levels in many foods.

Tryptophan is a chemical needed by the horse's body to form the neurotransmitter serotonin. Neurotransmitters are chemicals that carry signals in the horse's nervous system. In people, high levels of serotonin are found in the fluid around the brain during sleep in man. Giving high levels of tryptophan is supposed to cause high levels of serotonin and make horses feel "sleepy." This effect may be desired in some show horses.

Unfortunately, there are no studies to show that tryptophan has any effect on the horse. Anecdotal reports of its effectiveness vary from "great" to "worthless."

The *L* in L-tryptophan is a chemistry term that refers to its chemical configuration.

PRECAUTIONS   In man, tryptophan ingestion, even in fairly small amounts, has been associated with a blood disease called eosinophilia-myalgia. Thus, tryptophan supplements have been pulled from the human market. This condition has not as yet been reported in horses receiving this amino acid.

TURPENTINE

Turpentine is a light oil that is obtained from processing crude oil. Purified turpentine was used as a diuretic and antiparasitic agent in people many, many years ago. Newer and safer drugs have long since replaced the use of turpentine as a pharmaceutical.

In horses, turpentine is used primarily on the hoof and is a component of a variety of hoof dressings. It also is reported to be a toughening agent for the hoof, especially the sole.

There is an over-the-counter wound preparation that contains turpentine. What possible benefit could be obtained from putting turpentine on delicate, healing tissue escapes understanding.

· U ·

UREA

Urea is a nitrogen-containing compound that is found in urine. At one time, it was used as an oral diuretic in man but it is only used intravenously today.

Urea is a component of an over-the-counter dressing used on horse hooves. What purpose it might serve it unknown.

· V ·

VALIUM   (see Diazepam)

VASELINE   (see Petrolatum)

VENICE TURPENTINE   (see *Turpentine*)

VETALOG   (see *Triamcinolone*)

VITAMIN

Vitamin is a general term that is used to describe a variety of unrelated organic compounds that occur in most foods in small amounts. They are necessary for the normal metabolic functions of the body.

Vitamin deficiencies are not known to exist naturally in the horse. The horse's body provides all of its own vitamins (unlike humans), both by synthesis from the system and by absorption of vitamins produced by the bacteria that live in the gastrointestinal tract.

There appears to be no need for vitamin supplementation in the horse, according to most studies. However, all vitamins are available in relatively inexpensive forms and they are widely used. The rule seems to be: When in doubt, use vitamins. Fortunately, considering the frequency with which they are given, vitamins are safe supplements to give to horses and are only toxic in large doses.

VITAMIN A

Vitamin A maintains the normal structure and function of the epithelial cells, the surface cells that occur throughout the body. It is also needed for normal bone growth. It has a well-defined role in maintaining normal vision. Vitamin A is also needed for normal reproductive function in both males and females.

Deficiencies of vitamin A first show up as changes in the epithelial surfaces. Surfaces become dryer and less resilient; their mucus-secreting capacity becomes reduced. As epithelial surfaces lose their normal capabilities, the potential for infection increases.

Night blindness and excessive tear formation are ocular signs of vitamin A deficiencies. Reproductive efficiency is also greatly reduced.

It has been said that if the feed given to a horse has the color green in it, there is sufficient vitamin A for the needs of the horse. The amount of vitamin A in feed is roughly equal to the amount of the color green in the feed. Additionally, a three- to six-month supply of vitamin A is stored in the liver of the horse.

Vitamin and mineral supplements commonly contain vitamin A. Adding vitamin A supplements to mineral mixtures rapidly destroys the vitamin.

Vitamin A is one of the few vitamins that can cause toxicities. Fortunately, the dosages required for toxicities are quite large. The signs of toxicities are similar to those of deficiencies.

VITAMIN B

The B-vitamins are a whole group of vitamins with a variety of metabolic functions in the horse. They are found in plentiful supply in horse feed. The microorganisms of the horse's digestive tract also manufacture B-vitamins in large amounts. In normal horses, these two sources provide more than enough of the B-vitamins needed to meet the horse's requirements.

B-vitamins are among the most commonly supplemented vitamins in the horse, possibly because of the fact that in people, B-vitamin deficiencies occasionally occur. People do not get B-vitamins from the bacteria in their intestines and sometimes dietary sources are inadequate (in some vegetarian diets, for example). Hence, B-vitamin deficiencies are occasionally seen in people. The vitamin B story in people isn't necessarily the same as for horses, however.

B-vitamins are commonly given as a supplement to horses when they are in disease states. The B-vitamins are not stored in the horse's body for long periods of time. Chronic disease or decreased food intake may be considered reasons to provide B-vitamin supplementation to a horse. It is virtually impossible (and extremely expensive) to determine that a horse might be deficient in a specific B-vitamin, and supplements are relatively cheap; hence, frequently they are given "just in case" something might be needed.

It is commonly thought that B-vitamins can serve as an appetite stimulant. Experimental evidence with B-vitamins has shown no effect in stimulating the horse's appetite.

Sterile "vitamin B-complex" solutions are available for IM injection in the horse. These products typically contain vitamins B-I, B-2, B-3, B-6, pantothenic acid and B-12. Warnings on the label suggest caution because administration of vitamin B-I has resulted in anaphylactic (allergic) shock in some animals.

VITAMIN B-I *(Thiamine)*

Vitamin B-I is important in the production of energy by the cells of the horse's body. It is present in high levels in plant products, like hay. Interestingly, it is easily destroyed by heat and cooking, so thiamine may have to be added back to heat-processed feeds to restore preprocessing levels. Intestinal bacteria produce a great deal of thiamine. It is impossible to give a horse a normal diet that is thiamine deficient. Dietary thiamine deficiencies have only been seen in horses with experimentally produced diets.

Deficiencies of thiamine have been associated with the ingestion of plants that produce enzymes that break down thiamine or have antithiamine activity. Signs of thiamine deficiency include loss of appetite, weight loss, hemorrhage of the gums and heart rate abnormalities.

Thiamine toxicity is very unlikely if the vitamin is given orally. A dose of one thousand times that which is recommended appears to be safe.

High doses of thiamine have been injected into the horse in an effort to provide "natural" tranquilization. Indeed, some work done in Australia suggested that horses given thiamine seemed to be less excitable while walking to the racetrack. However, other studies have been unable to repeat this effect.

A negative side effect of thiamine is reported to be anaphylactic (allergic) shock. This effect is reportedly seen more often when the vitamin is given IV. Excessive blood levels of thiamine are prohibited by racing associations and the AHSA.

VITAMIN B-2   *(Riboflavin)*

Vitamin B-2, another vitamin important for normal metabolic activity in the horse, is also provided in high levels in horse feed and is produced by the bacteria of the horse's intestines. Neither deficiencies nor toxicities of vitamin B-2 have ever been reported in the horse.

VITAMIN B-3   *(Niacin)*

Niacin is important for energy production in all cells of the horse's body. As with all B-vitamins, the horse's normal intake and intestinal production appear to provide vast amounts of vitamin B-3 for the horse. Vitamin B-3 can also be manufactured from the amino acid tryptophan in the horse's tissues. Specific deficiencies or toxicities have not been reported in the horse.

VITAMIN B-6

Vitamin B-6 is actually a generic term for three similar compounds that have equal vitamin activity: pyridoxal, pyridoxine and pyridoxamine. No dietary requirements for these have been established in the horse and their precise functions are not known. Ample levels are provided from the normal sources in the horse. Deficiencies or toxicities of vitamin B-6 are unknown.

VITAMIN B-12 *(Cyanocobalamin)*

Vitamin B-12 is the only B-vitamin that is not found in large amounts in the horse's feed. However, synthesis of vitamin B-12 by the intestinal bacteria of the horse is more than adequate to meet the horse's needs, even when extremely low amounts of the vitamin are supplied in the diet. Vitamin B-12 is needed for red blood cells to mature. There are no reports of vitamin B-12 deficiencies or toxicities in the horse.

Vitamin B-12 is available as a sterile solution for IM or IV injection at a variety of concentrations. It is commonly used in an effort to pep up or "build blood" in horses that are deemed to be inadequate in these areas. There has been no observed response to vitamin B-12 injections in experimental situations. Injected B-12 is removed rapidly from the blood by the kidney and liver.

VITAMIN C

Also known as ascorbic acid, vitamin C is found in high levels in many vegetable compounds (like hay). It has a variety of important metabolic functions. Like vitamin E and the trace mineral selenium, vitamin C is also an anti-oxidant (see Vitamin E; Selenium).

Vitamin C deficiencies are unknown in horses because horses synthesize it in their bodies. In man, a deficiency of vitamin C causes scurvy, a condition characterized by weakness, anemia, spongy gums and a tendency towards bruising and bleeding. Supplemental vitamin C has no known beneficial effects in the horse.

VITAMIN D

Vitamin D is formed in the tissues of the horse by the action of the sun's rays on a by-product of the body's cholesterol. Because vitamin D levels are related to exposure to the sun, it is very difficult to make a horse deficient in vitamin D.

Vitamin D is stored in all tissues of the horse's body. It helps to maintain calcium and phosphorus levels in the body. Calcium and phosphorus are two minerals that are needed for bone formation (see Calcium, Phosphorus). Accordingly, vitamin D deficiencies, on the rare occasions that they are seen, occur in growing animals and show up as abnormalities of bone formation (rickets).

Vitamin D toxicity has been reported in horses. Most commonly it is associated with eating the wild jasmine plant (*Cestrum diurnum*), although there are reports of horses being given too much vitamin D in their diets. Signs of toxicity are stiffness and soreness, lack of eating, weight loss, excessive drinking and urination and calcification of the kidneys. The prognosis for recovery from vitamin D toxicosis is poor.

VITAMIN E

Vitamin E is necessary in the diet of the horse for normal reproduction, normal muscle development, normal red blood cell function and a variety of other biochemical functions. It is found in high levels in cereals, wheat germ oil and various grains.

Vitamin E is also an antioxidant. Antioxidant compounds prevent or delay the deterioration of substances when they are exposed to oxygen. Because of its antioxidant properties, vitamin E is frequently administered as treatment or prevention for acute or chronic equine exertional rhabdomyolysis, also known as tying up, myositis or azoturia. Theoretically, vitamin E would help prevent further degrading of muscle cells, as is seen with this condition. Typically, it is combined with selenium, a trace mineral, for treatment or prevention of this condition. No scientific evidence exists to support the effectiveness of this treatment for rhabdomyolysis, however.

Vitamin E is available in various ointments and oils for application to wounds in the horse. It is also found in various hoof dressings. There is no evidence that vitamin E has any effect in these areas. Application of vitamin E to the surface of a wound does not decrease the formation of scar tissue, nor does it increase the speed of or the amount of hair regrowth.

VITAMIN K

This group of vitamins promotes clotting of the blood by increasing the synthesis of one of the clotting factors (prothrombin) in the liver. High amounts of vitamin K occur in alfalfa hay. Vitamin K deficiencies are not known to occur in horses.

· W ·

WHEAT GERM OIL

Wheat germ oil is a plant oil that is often seen in health food stores. It is edible and contains various vitamins and fatty acids.

Wheat germ oil is also a component of various hoof dressings for the horse (see Hoof Dressings). It is presumably used for the same reasons as other plant oils such as linseed or coconut oils.

WHITE LOTION

White lotion is a mild solution of zinc sulfate. It is an astringent and a very mild antibacterial agent.

Some veterinarians use white lotion to treat skin diseases of the horse.

WINSTROL-V *(see Stanozolol)*

WINTERGREEN OIL *(see Methyl Salicylate)*

WITCH HAZEL

Witch hazel is a volatile liquid distilled from a plant. It has use as a mild astringent (see Astringent). It is also used as a mild counterirritant.

In horses, witch hazel is used in formulating a variety of liniment and coolant gel–type products that are sold over the counter. It has a very distinctive smell but little or no therapeutic value.

WORMWOOD OIL

Wormwood extracts come from an aromatic plant. The extract is bitter and is used in flavoring certain wines and in making absinthe, a green liqueur. In the 1800s, wormwood extract was also used to treat sprains.

Wormwood oil is found in a commonly used liniment preparation sold over the counter for horses (see Liniment). What effectiveness it might have is unknown.

WOUND TREATMENTS

Wounds of the horse are an unfortunate and somewhat common occurrence, since horses do seem to be accident-prone. Wounds that go deep through the skin surface and reveal or penetrate underlying structures should be treated by a veterinarian as rapidly as possible.

After wounds occur, horse owners want to generally clean them with a disinfectant solution such as chlorhexidine, povidone-iodine or hydrogen peroxide (see various headings). When done by the owner, the benefits obtained from cleaning wounds are more likely related to the mechanical removal of debris than to the particular solution that is chosen to do it.

Surface scrapes, those wounds that remove hair and/or cause reddening of the skin, rarely, if ever, require treatment of any kind. Horse owners, however, frequently feel that it is necessary to apply some sort of antibacterial, antibiotic or vitamin preparation to these areas to "help" healing. In truth, it is virtually impossible to do anything to prevent rapid healing of these superficial scrapes; treatment is often more for the horse owner than for the horse. There is also no treatment available that promotes or speeds hair growth on these superficial wounds.

After surgical repair of wounds, antibiotic wound dressings are frequently applied to the surface. In sutured wounds, however, a wound dressing may not be all that important. Many surgeons feel that a sutured wound doesn't need to be covered with any type of medicated dressing, as long as it is protected from additional trauma or contamination.

Finally, many different types of wound dressings are commonly applied to granulation tissue. Granulation tissue forms when the skin edges of a wound are too far apart to reunite with sutures, usually because of tissue loss. The appearance of granulation tissue is part of normal healing in these wounds. Horse owners, however, become greatly concerned about excessive granulation tissue, or "proud flesh."

"Proud flesh" describes granulation tissue that has grown beyond the surface of the wound. Once beyond the wound surface, granulation tissue can proliferate and look ugly. "Proud flesh" is not abnormal tissue, however. It is normal tissue that has been allowed to overgrow. It is not "bad" for a wound. It is not dangerous to the horse. Its presence does not mean that a horse will become permanently disfigured. It may mean that not enough attention has been paid to the wound, since there's no reason why a wound that has been properly cared for should develop "proud flesh."

It is occasionally necessary to control the growth of granulation tissue so that a wound can heal. The pressure from a properly applied bandage can help limit the growth of "proud flesh." The growth of this tissue can also be controlled by the use of corticosteroid-based ointments (see Corticosteroid). These ointments slow the growth of granulation tissue when they are applied to the surface of the tissue. When applied starting five days from the initial injury, corticosteroid ointments do not slow down the epithelial cells growing in from the sides of the wound. Excessive granulation tissue also can be cut back with a scalpel.

What should not be done to granulation tissue is to put substances on it that are caustic and damaging to the fresh tissue. Things like lime, kerosene, copper sulfate, sulfuric acid, pine tar or silver nitrate are awful things to put on fresh tissue (see various headings). Remember, granulation tissue is normal, healing tissue. It is trying to heal your horse's wound. Don't hurt it.

If you put caustic chemicals on the tissue, you will induce a chemical burn. The body will not heal over this newly damaged tissue until the damaged tissue itself has had time to heal. As wound treatments, these caustic agents cause a hard scab to form on tissue because they cause surface proteins to come out of solution (this action is called "precipitation"). Although they may kill bacteria directly, the formation of a chemical scab on healing tissue is not necessarily beneficial. In fact, the growth of bacteria may even be favored by the protection of the chemically caused scab.

Wounds will try to heal in spite of the wide variety of inappropriate substances applied to them. One rule of thumb used by some surgeons is that you should never put anything on a wound that you would not put in your own eye. It's not a bad rule to follow.

WYAMINE SULFATE

Wyamine is a drug used in man to increase blood pressure. In horses, some people have tried to use it as a stimulant to improve racing performance. Wyamine has not been tested on horses and its effects are unsubstantiated.

· X ·

XYLAZINE HYDROCHLORIDE   *Rompun, Anased*

Xylazine is a short-acting sedative for horses. It is also a potent analgesic, particularly for relief of abdominal pain (colic), and it is very commonly used for the control of colic pain. In fact, some clinicians feel that if a horse's abdominal pain cannot be controlled by xylazine, the problem most likely will require surgery to correct. Xylazine is also a relaxant of skeletal muscle. After the drug is given to the horse, the horse's head drops within a very short time, indicating that he is sedated.

Xylazine comes as a sterile liquid. It can be given IV or IM and its effects are dose related.

PRECAUTIONS   In large doses, xylazine can cause a horse to become unsteady. It is particularly important to note that even when horses are sedated with large doses of xylazine, they can still react to stimuli. Horses have been observed to kick out quickly, even while sedated with relatively large doses of this drug.

Horses intended for use in shows must not have traces of xylazine in their systems. Recommended withdrawal time by the AHSA is seventy-two hours prior to competition.

SIDE EFFECTS   After dosage with xylazine, it is common to observe a heart rhythm abnormality known as second degree A-V block. This is best described as the heart having a regular pattern, characterized by the heart rhythm slowing down and then skipping a beat. This usually disappears within a few minutes of administration of the drug and is not a health threat to the horse. Caution in giving the drug to horses with heart problems would be advisable, however.

Xylazine relaxes the muscles of the horse. It can reduce the respiratory rate, as is seen in natural sleep. Care should be taken in using xylazine in horses with depressed respiration.

Sweating is also common after administration of xylazine. This is an effect of the drug on sweat glands and is not a sign of an abnormal or dangerous response.

· Y ·

YUCCA

Yucca is a feed supplement that is purported to be for the relief of arthritic conditions of the horse. It is obtained from a cactuslike plant.

Most preparations are combined with anise, the seed that gives the flavoring to black licorice.

Herbal pharmacy texts give no information as to why yucca should be beneficial in the treatment of arthritis.

· Z ·

ZANTAC   *(see Ranitidine)*

ZINC

Zinc is a trace mineral that is an important part of many enzymes associated with skeletal development in the horse.

Zinc deficiencies have not been reported in horses. It is virtually impossible for a horse not to get enough zinc in his diet.

Zinc toxicity has been reported in horses, primarily where pastures have been contaminated from metal-smelting activity or where water has been contaminated by porous galvanized pipe. Bone and joint abnormalities have been identified in horses with zinc toxicity. Clinical signs of zinc intoxication include stiffness, lameness and joint swelling.

BIBLIOGRAPHY

Balch, J. F., and P. A. Balch. *Prescription for Nutritional Healing.* Garden Park City, N.Y.: Avery Publishing Group, 1990.

Barnum, R. C. *The People's Home Library.* Toronto: Imperial Publishing Company, 1916.

Bennett, K., ed. *Compendium of Veterinary Products,* 2nd ed. Port Huron, Mich.: North American Compendiums, Inc., 1993.

Booth, N. H., and L. E. McConals. *Veterinary Pharmacology and Therapeutics.* Ames, Iowa: Iowa State University Press, 1988.

Editors of the UC Berkeley "Wellness Letter." *The Wellness Encyclopedia.* New York: Houghton Mifflin Company, 1991.

Hinchcliff, K. W., and R. A. Sams, eds. "Drug Use in Performance Horses." *The Veterinary Clinics of North America, Equine Practice,* 9:3. Philadelphia: W. B. Saunders and Company, 1993.

Hintz, H. F., ed. "Clinical Nutrition." *The Veterinary Clinics of North America, Equine Practice,* 6:2. Philadelphia: W. B. Saunders and Company, 1990.

Jones, W. E. *Equine Sports Medicine.* Philadelphia: Lea & Febiger, 1989.

McKinnon, A. O., and J. L. Voss. *Equine Reproduction.* Philadelphia: Lea & Febiger, 1993.

National Research Council. *Nutrient Requirements of Horses,* 5th ed. Washington, DC: National Academy Press, 1989.

Osol, A., and J. E. Hoover. *Remington's Pharmaceutical Sciences.* Easton, Pa.: Mack Publishing Company, 1975.

Robinson, N. E., ed. *Current Therapy in Equine Medicine 3.* Philadelphia: W. B. Saunders and Company, 1992.

Robinson, N. E., ed. *Current Therapy in Equine Medicine 2.* Philadelphia: W. B. Saunders and Company, 1987.

White, N. A., and J. N. Moore. *Current Practice of Equine Surgery.* New York: J. B. Lippincott Company, 1990.

Index of Brand Names

Telmin, 43

Terramycin, 155

Torbugesic, 50

Tranquazine, 137

Tresaderm, 116

Triple Antibiotic Ointment, 40,
    116, 131

Twin-Pen, 124–25

U

Up-Tite (poultice), 134

V

Valium, 72

Vaseline, 127

Vetadine, 135

Vetalar, 103

Vetalog, 157

Vetrolin, 107

Vetropolycin, 131

Virosan, 57

VitaHoof, 91

W

Winstrol-V, 149

Wonder Dust (wound treatment),
    169–71

Z

Zantac, 143

Zimectrin, 101